"Erlanger A. Turner's *Raising Resilient Black Kids* is a practical guide for t
It answers so many of the questions my clients ask about *how* to have th
to develop in the face of racism, but this workbook helps everyone in
process their own feelings and experiences to support healthy and thr....... ...., ...
youth."

> —**Riana Elyse Anderson, PhD, LCP**, associate professor of social work and
> clinical psychology at Columbia University, and developer and director of
> the EMBRace Program

"This workbook is an essential resource for parents navigating the complexities of racial stress with their children. Through practical guidance and insights, it empowers parents to foster resilience, emotional intelligence, and empowerment in their children. This book equips parents and caregivers with tools to navigate challenging conversations, build self-esteem, and cultivate a strong sense of identity. A must-read for anyone committed to supporting Black children's well-being and emotional success."

> —**Allen Eugene Lipscomb, PsyD, LCSW**, associate professor and associate
> chair of social work at California State University, Northridge; and author of
> *Bonding Recognition Understanding and Healing (BRuH) Approach*

"*Raising Resilient Black Kids* is an excellent conversation starter. Both as a tool for caregivers to begin racism-related conversations with their children and, importantly, to help caregivers start an internal conversation about their own experiences navigating racism. Turner does an amazing job of offering accessible, developmentally appropriate conversational tools for caregivers. I will definitely be recommending the book's exercises to many Black families in my clinical practice."

> —**Ryan C.T. DeLapp, PhD**, director of the Racial, Ethnic, And Cultural
> Healing (REACH) Program at the Ross Center

"Discover strategies to help children navigate racial stress and thrive in *Raising Resilient Black Kids* by Earl Turner. I appreciate the author's intentionality in providing culturally affirming, evidence-based strategies for parents to support their children's emotional well-being and resilience. Activities in the book can be used not only for individuals, but also for group settings. This book is a valuable resource for Black families."

> —**Shanita Brown, PhD, LCMHC, NCC**, teaching assistant professor at
> East Carolina University

"What a joy to review this accessible, engaging book written specifically for Black parents! Turner's compassionate guidance provides Black parents with information, tools, and gentle encouragement to support them in preparing Black children to thrive in the context of racism. He is both friend and expert. The inclusion of empowering, child-friendly activism activities, mindfulness skills to manage reactivity, and attention to spirituality make this a unique and valuable resource."

> —**Shelly P. Harrell, PhD**, professor of psychology at Pepperdine University Graduate School of Education and Psychology, and licensed psychologist in independent practice

"*Raising Resilient Black Kids* is filled with useful resources, worksheets, and journal prompts to help parents understand racial stress and navigate 'the race talk' with their children. Through the HEAL method, Turner provides clear and practical techniques for parents to support their children's mental health. This book is a must-read for parents of Black kids!"

> —**Celeste M. Malone, PhD, MS**, associate professor of school psychology at Howard University, and past president of the National Association of School Psychologists

"Earl Turner has truly provided readers with a gift with this publication. I know firsthand the stressors associated with parenting Black youth as a mother and as a psychologist who collaborates with patients through the parenting process. I am incredibly excited to have a resource like this one to use with my clients in sessions, recommend for them to use at home, and as a tool in my own toolbox as a Black mental health expert and mother of two Black children."

> —**Raquel Martin, PhD**, assistant professor and scientist at Tennessee State University, licensed clinical psychologist, podcast host, and Black mental health expert

Raising Resilient Black Kids

A PARENT'S GUIDE TO HELPING CHILDREN COPE WITH RACIAL STRESS, MANAGE EMOTIONS & THRIVE

ERLANGER A. TURNER, PHD

New Harbinger Publications, Inc.

Publisher's Note

NEW HARBINGER PUBLICATIONS is a registered trademark of New Harbinger Publications, Inc.

New Harbinger Publications is an employee-owned company.

Cover design by Sara Christian

Acquired by Wendy Millstine and Jennye Garibaldi

Edited by Karen Schader

Printed in the United States of America

26   25   24

10   9   8   7   6   5   4   3   2   1   First Printing

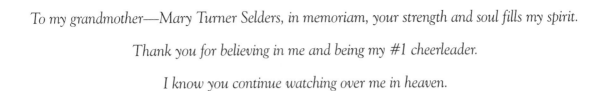

To my grandmother—Mary Turner Selders, in memoriam, your strength and soul fills my spirit.

Thank you for believing in me and being my #1 cheerleader.

I know you continue watching over me in heaven.

Contents

Foreword

As a Black mother and a Black psychologist, one of my highest honors has been to raise my children Ife and Ayo. Following the tradition of my African American parents, we gave them African names. Their Nigerian names mean "love" and "joy." Each time their name is called by family, friends, strangers, and community members, it is a reminder to them of their true essence, their sacred cultural identity. Naming can be an affirming, empowering act of identification. Resilience, or bouncing back, requires children know who they are so they can always return to the truth of themselves.

I am delighted that my colleague and friend, Dr. Erlanger Turner, one of the noteworthy child and adolescent psychologists of our time, has authored *Raising Resilient Black Kids* in a time when parents urgently need this resource. You made the right choice in selecting this book to nourish your parental journey. I want to share with you some of the key components Dr. Turner explores in this book to prepare and equip you for the resource-rich road ahead.

Dr. Turner makes the significant argument for parents and, in a developmentally appropriate way, their children to be aware of the realities of racial stress and trauma. Racism doesn't wait until adulthood to reveal itself. It shows up on playgrounds, in classrooms, in religious settings, at amusement parks, and in the media. Children, and Black kids in particular, are given messages that convey notions of inferiority, dehumanization, and unworthiness. Parents of Black kids must be aware of this to protect, preserve, and heal the self-esteem and self-efficacy of their children. Parents must be intentional in recognizing the impact of racism on their children and themselves. The effects seen in children, according to the scientific literature, can include depression, anxiety, anger, distrust, difficulty sleeping, and hopelessness. Not only do we want to recognize racism, but also practice resisting it and teaching your child that they have power to resist it. Acts of resistance may include starting a petition, attending a march, writing a complaint, donating money or other resources to a racial justice or antiracism initiative, creating art that explores liberation, or seeking a leadership role to help disrupt systemic racism. Racism is real *and* you, your children, and the larger community can work together to dismantle it.

To counteract racism, parents of Black children have to be intentional about positive racial socialization, as Dr. Turner describes. This positive messaging about the beauty, brilliance, talent, values, and cultural richness of Black people can be conveyed through exposure to Black arts and culture from parents, faith communities, cultural enrichment programs, media, and books written about and for Black children. I gave my children what my parents gave me. This included opportunities to connect in spaces where they were not the only one. Predominantly Black spaces become sites of resilience building by communicating to Black children that a community of care and investment in their possibility exists.

Another important aspect Dr. Turner covers is the importance of self- and community care for parents of Black kids. Trying to protect and prepare your children is an ongoing process that can have devastating risks of psychological and physical harm. It is important for your children to get the most nourished, rested, grounded version of you. When we are highly anxious or despairing, our children can become aware of this and either take on these same symptoms or become a worried, parentified child who feels responsible for the well-being of their parent. I encourage you to find ways to refill your well and to refill it often, not just once you are burned out. Refilling your well can include eating healthy meals, getting exercise, spending time outside in the sun, nourishing your mutually beneficial friendships, engaging in spiritual practices, going to therapy, and participating in creative expressions such as music or dance. Along with self-care, community care is important. It can be a vital lifeline to have other friends who are raising Black kids. You can be a practical and psychological resource for each other, sharing wins and challenges to celebrate and comfort you.

While the challenges due to racism, and other developmental challenges, can be a pervasive reality, so is the very real opportunity to raise children who thrive. In your parenting, please consider a vision beyond survival mode. Yes, you want your children to survive, but they are worthy of so much more. Your children come from a heritage of people who overcame insurmountable odds and outlasted deadly circumstances. They survived and became thought leaders, inventors, creatives, and educators. This same possibility exists within your child. Without pressure, praise your children and remind them of their possibility with an awareness that there is purpose for their lives.

Finally, this thought-provoking book will give you some key concepts from mindfulness. Mindfulness means paying attention in the present moment, without judgment and with self-compassion. As parents of Black children, we can be hard on ourselves and harsh with our children. This perfectionism or judgment is often a result of exhaustion and anxiety. I hope you will create a soft landing for yourself and become a soft place for your children to land and know they will be met with care, love, and support. Despite the challenges, may you and your children rest, restore, rise, and shine.

—Thema Bryant, PhD
    Professor of psychology, Pepperdine University
    Author of *Homecoming: Overcome Fear and Trauma to Reclaim Your Whole Authentic Self*

Introduction

Racial discrimination is a daily encounter for many Black people whether you live in the suburbs or inner city. For decades, society has treated us and our children unfairly due to our race. It's no surprise that those harmful experiences that arise from prejudice and bias can cause stress and mental health problems.

As a psychologist, I work with children and their families to help them cope with exposure to racism and racial violence, which both can lead to racial stress. This type of stress can result from racist encounters that are emotionally taxing or that are perceived to threaten well-being (Harrell 2000). Despite some improvements in civil rights, there have been increases in anti-Black racism and police brutality against our community. According to a national survey published by the Pew Research Center (2023), 83 percent of Black adults said that efforts to ensure equality haven't gone far enough, and they think it's unlikely that there will be racial equality in their lifetime. This racial inequality can influence how you think about yourself and how you talk—or avoid talking—with your child to help them process these negative experiences.

Racism can be unsettling for parents and make you concerned about your child's mental health. Given that racial discrimination is so common, you probably know from personal experiences or from people you know that those injustices often result in psychological distress or racial stress. Racial stress in children can show up as anger, sadness, anxiety, behavior problems, or increased alertness to threats to their racial identity (Jones and Neblett 2017).

More explicit and direct forms of racism have become increasingly apparent. For example, more schools are teaching children that slavery was beneficial to our ancestors, or have dress codes that prevent Black children from wearing natural hair, such as locs. It is clear that having intentional conversations with children about race and racism is important. In my experience, parents often seek advice and tools on topics such as: "When should I talk with my child about race?" "What information should I bring up?" and "How can I help my child cope when they see racism?" These are the many questions that I hope this workbook will help you address as a parent (or caregiver) of a Black child.

Why I Wrote This Workbook

In the United States, Black people have experienced racial oppression and racism for centuries, and both continue to exist within many systems we use, including schools, parks and other community spaces, and health care settings. Most of us know this from our own families and experiences of our ancestors. Unfortunately, at times it seems that racism will never go away. This workbook is intended to provide you with strategies to help you provide a safe space to work through difficult experiences and conversations with your child in the comfort of your own home.

In the summer of 2020, the renewed need for a book like this came to prominence. After the murders of Breonna Taylor and George Floyd, many Black families were faced with the racial reckoning and its impact on our emotional, physical, and spiritual well-being. As communities took to the streets to protest, many parents like yourself were confronted with the dilemma of discussing race and racism with their child. I spent considerable amounts of time answering important questions such as "Do I take my child to a protest?" or "How does seeing racial violence affect my child's mental health?" *Raising Resilient Black Kids* is intended to help you navigate challenging topics like these with your child.

This workbook is a true labor of love. I have always been invested in improving the lives of youth and supporting their mental health through applying psychological research. This book will improve your understanding of the psychology of racism and your ability to help your child navigate racism to reduce difficulties that may shape their social and emotional development. As a guide, it will help you (a) explore the psychological impacts of racism on your child, (b) engage in self-exploration about your own experiences with discrimination and understand how those have shaped your parenting practices, and (c) identify practical strategies to manage emotions and promote resilience in your child.

The HEAL Method

The HEAL method—**healing emotions** and **anxiety** through **liberation**—is intended to be a simple guide that empowers you to build on your inherent skills that have allowed Black people to maintain our hopefulness about the future despite the enduring nature of racism.

This method offers you strategies to understand your child's unique experiences, equip them with the tools to process racial discrimination, and prepare them to move forward, while minimizing the negative influence of racism on their mental health and well-being.

Racism occurs in society and can influence how children think, feel, and behave. For example, for some children experiencing racism will cause internalized racism, poor self-esteem, anger, or racial stress. Chapter 1 will take a deeper dive into how racism and discrimination can affect your child.

The HEAL method combines principles from three different psychological approaches—*cognitive behavioral therapy* (CBT), *racial socialization*, and *liberation psychology*—to identify simple strategies that will help promote resilience in your child and prepare them to confront racial bias and oppression, while also offering strategies to promote liberation after experiencing racism in society.

CBT involves exploring the connections between our thoughts, feelings, and behaviors. CBT-based strategies can be used to help you and your child confront unhealthy thoughts that may lead to emotions such as sadness and anxiety. Some kids may internalize messages from society about their race that can lead to anxiety or depression; for example, messages such as, "People don't think I can be smart because I'm Black" or "Some kids at school make fun of my hair texture." Although these experiences are not universal, when these types of negative experiences dominate messages in society (through media, school, or community) they can be harmful to your child's self-esteem and emotional development. It is my hope that this workbook will provide tools for you to understand messages your child has received and to discover how you can help them challenge unhealthy or negative thoughts about their identity, with the objective being to reduce racial stress and increase their potential to thrive.

This workbook also uses racial socialization practices to help you have the race talk with your child. Racial socialization is the process of communicating messages about one's race and cultural heritage to help youth cope with discrimination (Jones and Neblett 2019). Racism is one of the hardest topics a parent can discuss with their child. Given the difficulties of this talk, many parents choose to avoid having these conversations, especially with young children. That may have been your decision before picking up this workbook, and your hesitation is understandable. Being worried about having this conversation can be rooted in your own fear and discomfort about introducing the topic to your child. That being said, one thing to remember is that the earlier you have this talk with your child, the better they will be at openly discussing race and taking pride in their racial identity.

Finally, the workbook applies principles from liberation psychology to help promote coping and healing. Liberation psychology involves "breaking the chains of personal oppression" and "transforming oppressive social structures through collective action" (Freire 1994; Moane 2003). This approach recognizes the multiple aspects of life that shape an individual's reality; promotes critical thinking; inspires creative expression; and fosters a sense of agency—that is, the ability to make choices that affect their lives. From the liberation psychology perspective, people are encouraged to "make things happen as opposed to allowing things to happen to them" (Bryant-Davis and Moore-Lobban 2020; Torres Rivera and Comas-Díaz 2020). In the context of the HEAL method, it will be important to help your child use problem solving and critical thinking to explore how to combat racism through activism.

To this end, the workbook uses the HEAL method to provide strategies that will empower you and your child to use your strengths, abilities, and lived experience to foster wellness and liberation to thrive in society while navigating experiences of racism, oppression, and discrimination. By acknowledging how historical oppression and racism affect you and your child, and processing those experiences, this workbook will offer tools to help promote resilience in your child.

My hope is that this workbook will help you understand that racism does not always have to leave a lasting scar on your child. You may fear that your child will witness or encounter racism that will leave a lasting negative impact on them, such as developing depression or distrust of all non-Black people. Some parents may even fear that their child will become hopeless about their future. One of your main jobs as a parent is to raise your child to grow up to be a healthy adult. I believe that an important part of that process is instilling in your child the certainty that while racism is bad, none of us should internalize those negative messages from society about our identity. When kids begin to believe these negative perceptions from others, it can be harmful to their emotional and mental health. However, by processing racial discrimination with your child and giving them the tools to liberate themselves from those negative perceptions, you can help them thrive.

How to Use This Workbook

This workbook is primarily geared toward parents of Black and African American youth. It will provide tools that parents across the African diaspora can use to help their child thrive. The content may also apply to therapists or clinicians who provide interventions with Black children.

The introduction and chapter 1 will serve as the general foundation to help you understand the impact of racism and discrimination on Black children. Given the role of oppression and racism on mental health outcomes, it is necessary to understand what situations and experiences elevate the risk of racial stress and how adverse childhood experiences (for example, witnessing police brutality) can lead to anxiety, depression, or adjustment difficulties. Therefore, these foundational sections will also offer some exercises and questions for you to explore so you can gauge how you and your child are emotionally affected by racism.

In chapters 2 through 5, you'll learn a series of techniques and complete activities based on CBT, racial socialization, and liberation psychology. Each chapter will begin with an overall discussion of the psychological science and then walk you through a series of activities that you and your child can explore together. The "Ask Dr. Earl" segments throughout the book will offer some advice for you based on questions frequently asked by parents. The workbook will also share some of my own experiences as a psychologist and offer some case examples to help you better understand the concepts you'll be reading about. The chapters will integrate practical tools and exercises for you to engage in with your child to help them navigate racist incidents. These activities are meant to help your child learn how to practice skills to cope and alleviate emotional stress. You might want to do some of them more than once, and you'll find PDF copies of many of the worksheets at the website for this book: http://www.newharbinger.com/53011. Finally, the chapters will conclude with a section that encourages you to take a moment to reflect on the materials and identify key learnings.

I often hear from parents about how there is a lack of resources available to help their child deal with experiences such as oppression and racism. While there is often an understanding of having the race talk, there are limited self-help books available to you as a Black parent. This workbook will not only provide the psychological principles that serve as the foundation for promoting healing and coping, but it will also offer practical strategies and tools you can use with your child.

Life is busy, so I don't expect you to pick up this workbook and complete every chapter week by week until you get to the end. One of the benefits of working through this in your home is the ability to go at your own pace.

One of the most important components of this book is practicing the skills and completing the journal prompts, so take your time reading the workbook, responding to the prompts, and practicing the strategies. The book provides space for you to write your responses; you can also choose to keep track of your responses in a separate journal. The workbook is designed to allow you to complete one chapter and then build on the information you have learned before progressing to the next chapter. Once you've understood the material in the entire workbook, you can refer back to specific sections as needed. At times, events that happen in society or your community may prompt you to review certain chapters. For example, if your child experiences racism at school after you've read the workbook, it may be helpful to revisit chapter 1 to review the conversation starters so you can check in with your child about that experience.

The more you work through the strategies, the easier it will be for you to use them and to know where to find resources in the workbook when needed. One of the best ways to learn a new skill is through action. My goal is to offer practical strategies in this workbook that will foster healing and resilience to help your child thrive in a racist society.

CHAPTER 1

Understanding Racial Stress and Your Child

As Black people, we understand the impact of racism based on knowledge of our ancestors or what we have experienced in our own lives. For example, you may have been racially profiled by the police while driving or by a store clerk while shopping in the mall. As a parent of Black child, you are an expert on racial discrimination in many ways. Even before you decided to pick up this workbook, you had an understanding of how racism affected you and your child. You know how your child emotionally responds to racial discrimination. They may have shut down at times, had problems sleeping, or told you their worries about what is happening in the community. You also know that your child is a sponge and often consumes information about you and their surroundings. If they see you get upset after witnessing racial violence, they may mirror some of your emotions, such as hurt or anger. One thing I often share with parents is the idea that you know your child and you know when things are not going well for them. It's your parent's intuition. Sometimes you might ignore those thoughts or feelings when you think your child is upset. At other times you may check in with your child to make sure everything is okay. What is important for you to remember is that when you recognize that something seems off with your child, don't ignore it. Instead, assess the situation and take action to better understand what is going on in your child's internal world.

Having a better understanding of how racism affects your child emotionally can help you know the best way to respond to them and help them be more resilient. In order to minimize the risk of poor mental health after being exposed to racial discrimination, one step is to process with your child how they perceive or make sense of the world. This knowledge about how your child understands these events will also help you better identify what thoughts your child is having, as well as what emotions they are experiencing.

In this chapter, you will

- learn how racism and discrimination impacts Black youth;

- develop an understanding of what factors may lead to racial stress and trauma; and

- explore ways to connect with your child to better understand their capacity to cope with experiences of racism in society.

Racial Discrimination in Society

Although racial discrimination frequently occurs within society and in our communities, it can be difficult to recognize how much it impacts Black children. Some research indicates that Black youth experience at least one incident of racism over the course of any given year. According to one recent study, Black youth experience racial discrimination or racial microaggressions on average at least five times per day (Lavner et al. 2022). You may be alarmed to realize that either your child or someone they know is experiencing racism daily.

Within the school environment, racism is also an unfortunate occurrence. In the last few years, you may have seen on the local or national news how Black kids experience being called racial slurs, are not allowed to participate in sports events due to their natural hair, and have been told by their peers that they don't want to be seated next to them because of their race. Of course, this is a problem—and it can also be seen as a public health issue. Based on what science tells us, the more children experience incidents of racial discrimination, the more they are at risk for psychological difficulties such as anxiety, depression, and trauma reactions (Anderson, Heard-Garris, and DeLapp 2022).

Keep in mind how your child generally responds when they are upset. You know your child. If your child comes home seeming angry, sad, or upset, I encourage you to take a moment to check in with them. Later in the chapter I will share some conversation starters that may be helpful for you to use when checking in with your child.

Unfortunately, racial discrimination can occur in many different settings, placing your child at risk of being exposed indirectly and directly. One of the most common places where children experience racial discrimination is at school. Black children experience racism indirectly by witnessing mistreatment of their peers by other students or school staff. They may also have direct exposure to racism in the form of name calling, personal attacks on their racial identity or culture, and racial biases when their teachers make comments about their ability to be successful on school tasks. When Black children are targets of racism and discrimination, it can result in negative consequences other than just psychological and emotional. According to the Southern Poverty Law Center (2019), when children experience racism in school, nine out of ten school administrators fail to appropriately address the situation or affirm the school's values of inclusion, potentially leading to racial stress that may also affect your child's ability to focus at school and be successful academically.

Another significant issue for our Black kids is community violence and police brutality. While we have seen increases in the awareness of police brutality due to the use of smartphones and technology, this concern is not new. However, your child may be more likely to be exposed to this type of community violence these days because technology has made it possible for the rapid sharing of videos and news (Bryant-Davis and Moore-Lobban 2020; Turner, Jernigan-Noesi, and Metzger 2021). I often encourage parents to be mindful that their child may be exposed to police brutality, either through watching the television news with you or by attending protests. While exposing your child to events that are happening is not necessarily a problem, you should consider that your child might be triggered. If you do decide to allow your child to watch the news coverage of these events or attend peaceful protests, be sure to take some time to process the experience with them.

Later in the book, I will talk more about ways to help your child if protests become violent or unsafe. For now, it's helpful to keep in mind that you should have a plan for supporting your child. Support might look like talking with your child before going to a protest or having a code word you can use to remind the child to cover their eyes or ears. In the end, it's important to remember that when kids have the opportunity to share their perspectives and have healthy conversations about racial discrimination, it can help reduce the potential negative impact on their well-being.

These questions can help you think about how you and your child have dealt with racial discrimination. You can use your journal or the blank lines to write down your answers.

Describe an incident where your child saw or experienced discrimination.

_____

_____ !

_____

_____

_____

_____

What was your child's response?

_____

_____

What was your response?

_____

_____

Would you respond differently if this incident happened today?

_____

_____

_____

_____

The Effects of Historical and Contemporary Racism

Racism is embedded in the fabric of American society. From America's inception as a nation to the present day, Black people have been marginalized and subjected to racial discrimination. Historically, enslaved African people helped build this nation but were denied many rights, including the ability to get married or obtain an education. Racism has been defined as differential treatment of individuals based upon their skin color, and it often results in restricted access to goods, services, and opportunities. Physician and public health expert Camara P. Jones (2000) describes different levels of racism that exist in society, including individual (involving one person or a small group of people) and structural (involving policies and laws that lead to oppression and marginalization).

As Black people, we understand that our ancestors experienced racism in the forms of being enslaved, being segregated within society, and victimized by racial violence. You may also have directly or indirectly witnessed how racism and discrimination impacted your community on multiple levels; for example, over-representation of Black people within the legal system, harsher punishment of our children within schools, and inadequate treatment within health care systems.

In more recent years, you may have seen where societal and institutional racism has led to marginalization of youth within school systems, and how it has impacted access to mental health care within your community. For example, in some schools there are policies that prevent our kids from wearing their hair naturally. As a parent, you can be emotionally affected by all of these situations. They can also contribute to how you care for your child. For instance, you may experience anger and sadness when you observe racial violence or discrimination toward children. Those experiences can also trigger strong emotions, and the thought of talking with your child about racism may feel like a far-fetched idea. If this is how you've felt, it may have caused you to avoid talking with your child about racial discrimination. On the other hand, you may have made the decision to be more intentional about having the race talk with your child. Either way, I applaud you for honoring your feelings in that moment to take care of yourself and your child.

Your Personal Experiences

Take a moment to consider your personal experiences with racism and discrimination. This self-reflection will help you understand how your experiences may have been similar to, or different from, those of other Black people.

What forms of racial discrimination have you experienced since becoming a parent?

_____

_____

How do you think racism in society has influenced your parenting? For example, are you fearful of discussing this with your child or have you confronted it directly?

_____

_____

_____

_____

_____

What first comes to mind when you think about having the race talk with your child?

_____

_____

What emotions do you feel when you think about having the race talk with your child?

_____

_____

What would be the main reason for you to decide to have the race talk with your child?

_____

_____

• *The Case of Jordan*

Kevin and Lauren are the parents of Jordan, an eight-year-old African American boy who lives in a large urban city. Recently, the TV news reported on an incident at a local school where the school resource officer was physically aggressive toward a Black student. Jordan's parents realized that this was the same school their son attended. According to the news, the child refused to open their backpack to show that they hadn't stolen their classmate's textbook. The officer assumed the child was engaging in criminal activity without giving them the benefit of doubt.

Kevin and Lauren were aware of these types of situations happening but never this close to home. They were physically upset by the images shown. However, their child had never mentioned any negative or racially motivated experiences to them. In order to protect Jordan's childhood innocence, they decided they would not have the race talk. Instead, they would continue monitoring the situation at school and revisit a possible conversation with Jordan in the future.

In this scenario, Jordan's parents were emotional after witnessing the racially motivated violence on the news. They learned that the resource officer was fired after being investigated for this behavior. While they seemed fearful that their son could have a similar experience, they didn't want to have him on alert. Kevin and Lauren avoided talking to Jordan about the incident to manage their own feelings and because they didn't want to promote mistrust and fear in him.

I can understand their thought process and commend them for making the best decision at that time for their family. On the other hand, it's important to recognize that this choice may be helpful only in the short run. By avoiding the race discussion, they helped reduce Jordan's distress in that moment. However, in the long run, this avoidance won't prepare Jordan to cope or confront racial discrimination down the road.

This is an opportunity for you to consider how this family handled the situation and how you might deal with similar experiences with your child. Take a moment to think, and then write down your answers.

Do you think it's a good idea to talk with an eight-year-old about racial violence? If not, what would be a good age to have these conversations?

_____

_____

As a parent, how do you think you would have handled the situation with Jordan? What would you have done differently than Kevin and Lauren did?

_____

_____

_____

What advice would you give Kevin and Lauren about talking with their child when he is older?

_____

_____

_____

It can be scary to talk with your child about racial discrimination, but it's important to remember that children can be resilient if you actively foster resilience in them. It is necessary to give your child the skills to navigate these harmful experiences during childhood so they can be resilient and well-adjusted in the face of racism. Whether you have had the race talk before or want to learn how to approach it with your child, I hope that this workbook gives you the confidence to take the best action for your child. Obviously there is no perfect way to work through these types of things but the strategies you'll learn here can help your child cope and thrive in the face of racism.

Ask Dr. Earl

A parent asks...

My son heard the teacher using a racial slur toward another student in his class. When he came home and told me, I was in shock. Will this exposure to racial discrimination cause emotional problems for him?

And I answer...

While there is no clear answer to this question, it is important to know that there are several possible ways children may respond to these types of situations. It is possible that your child will be well-adjusted after the incident. He could return to school and not be affected emotionally. On the other hand, your child may be worried about how the teacher may treat him or other students who look like him.

It's important to talk with your child about situations like this and reassure him that the behavior was not acceptable. Praise him for being honest by informing you about what happened to his classmate. I encourage you to maintain an open dialogue with your child following something like this, periodically asking if things have been going okay at school. This openness will help build trust and a supportive environment in your family.

Good communication is necessary to promote resilience. Communicating with your child about the potential to experience racism and bias helps them recognize that they are not the problem, so that when they witness or experience these events, they don't internalize these negative messages about their identity. Part of being resilient is overcoming negative experiences. If your child is not provided with an environment to talk about what is happening in their life, they may keep those feelings and thoughts to themselves. By having open communication, you offer a supportive environment to help your child express themselves and get the support that helps build resilience.

Exposure to Current Racial Violence and Discrimination

While historical racism can have long-lasting impacts on your child, it is also important to be mindful of exposure to current racial discrimination. Racism can affect children in a number of ways and understanding how it is transmitted can help you protect your child. Research has shown that exposure to traumatic events such as racial discrimination may impact children beyond immediate exposure within their community (Tynes et al. 2019). For example, when there are incidents of Black men and women killed by police out of your local area, children may be indirectly exposed to this information through television or social media apps, such as TikTok or Instagram. If you're viewing this content at home and your child is present, it may be helpful to minimize the likelihood that they are also viewing it. You may even take steps to avoid viewing this content in their presence. Technology plays a huge role in our lives, and you should be mindful of how media exposure to racial violence and discrimination can have a negative influence on your child's well-being.

You should be ready to respond if your child happens to come in contact with racism or discrimination indirectly. In this case, it will be helpful to talk with your child about the topic to understand how they are feeling. It will also be important to help your child realize that they have positive aspects to their identity and should not accept hate from others based on their identity. In chapter 3 of the workbook, we'll talk more about building resilience through racial socialization.

These questions can help you process how indirect exposure to racism affects your child.

What exposure has your child had to racism through television or social media?

_____

_____

_____

_____

_____

_____

How has your child typically reacted to this exposure?

_____

_____

_____

How have you discussed racism with your child?

_____

_____

_____

What fears do you have about your child witnessing or being exposed to racial discrimination and violence?

_____

_____

_____

_____

If your child is exposed to racism through television or social media, how will you help them manage their emotions?

_____

_____

_____

Minimizing Indirect Exposure to Racial Violence

Whether we use social media to stay in contact with family or friends, or to stay up-to-date on current events, most of us spend some portion of our day on our smartphone or tablet. While these devices enhance our lives in many ways, they also pose the risk of increased exposure to negative events such as racial discrimination when they are used in the presence of children. To help reduce exposure, some families limit their children's access to devices, or don't allow it at all. Children in other families may have a tablet or smartphone for playing games, watching YouTube, or engaging with educational content. In both cases, there is a possibility that at some point children may be indirectly exposed to racism, bias, or injustice, so it is important that you take steps like these to reduce this risk:

- Turn on your sensitive content setting on social media.

- Review websites and online content before your child is given access.

- Identify a safe time during the day to browse your devices when children are not around.

- Avoid watching distressing news on television or smartphones with your child.

- Monitor and adjust setting on your child's devices to limit exposure to racism.

These suggestions can help you minimize online exposure to racial discrimination, but you should still be prepared to support your child in case they are exposed to bias or discrimination. Chapters 2 and 3 will provide some strategies to help you and your child cope. However, for now it is important to remember to remain calm in the presence of your child—taking a moment to engage in some slow deep breathing can help—and to step away from the content that may be triggering.

Symptoms of Racial Stress

Racial stress is often described as a psychological or emotional reaction to encounters of racial harassment, witnessing racial violence, and experiencing types of discrimination, such as public humiliation due to your natural hair (Harrell 2000; Turner 2019). While racial stress is not a formal mental health diagnosis, it does involve many different emotional and behavioral reactions. Symptoms may include being anxious or worried, experiencing elevated levels of sadness, fearing mistreatment by those outside your racial group, or feelings of anger.

It is important to recognize when your child exhibits a psychological reaction to stressful racial encounters, and being aware of the typical responses to racial discrimination can help you better support your child after those difficult experiences. It is only natural for humans to have an emotional response to situations that attack us physically or mentally. These reactions may include symptoms that affect children's emotions, thinking, behaviors, and social interactions.

Common Symptoms of Racial Stress

Take a look at the list of common symptoms that you or your child may experience following direct or indirect exposure to racial discrimination. Use the middle column to check off the symptoms you've personally experienced, and the righthand column for the symptoms you've witnessed your child experience. This exercise will give you an idea about how racism has impacted your family.

Emotional Symptoms		
	I've experienced	My child has experienced
Frustration		
Irritability		
Sadness		
Anxiety		
Behavioral Symptoms		
Expressions of anger		
Lack of interest in activities		
Isolating		
Being clingy toward loved ones		

Cognitive Symptoms		
	I've experienced	My child has experienced
Increased negative thinking		
Decreased self-esteem		
Internalized racism		
Social Symptoms		
Avoiding interactions with non-Black peers/adults		
Decreased trust toward white people		
Difficulties getting along with others		

• The Case of Melanie

Melanie is a ten-year-old African American girl growing up in a middle-class community. The school she attends has a mix of people from different racial and ethnic groups. Her parents have always encouraged her to love her race and culture.

One day while Melanie was playing with her friends at recess, the coach, who was white, asked if she wanted to join the cheerleading squad for the local recreational sports team. She was excited because she loved dancing. She was looking forward to cheering for the team and learning new dance routines. After her parents gave her permission to sign up, they attended the informational meeting about joining the squad.

At the meeting, the kids went into the gym to learn some basic choreography while the parents were given information. After the practice, the coach called Melanie over and told her that she couldn't wear her hair in afro-puffs. Melanie was embarrassed and didn't tell anyone about what happened. She didn't even tell her parents. When she got home, she immediately went to her room and laid on her bed in silence. Her parents noticed her mood but they assumed she was just tired from practice.

Over the next few weeks, she avoided going to practice and repeatedly told her parents "I'm not feeling well" or "I have a stomachache." Eventually Melanie told her parents that she didn't want to cheer anymore. They decided that it was her choice to participate or not, and they agreed to support her with finding another activity.

In this scenario, Melanie exhibited several symptoms of racial stress following her encounter with her coach about her hair. Some of the symptoms you may have observed include isolation, sadness, decreased self-esteem, and avoiding interactions with her white coach. One important thing to recognize about this situation is that, at first, she did not tell her parents what had happened. As a result, her parents were not aware of how she was struggling.

Children sometimes hide hurtful experiences because they don't want to disappoint their parent(s). Frequently checking in on your child and asking direct questions about their daily life is extremely important. This practice will help foster a strong relationship and build an environment of open communication. Having open communication with your child provides a space for you to read between the lines when they attempt to shield you from being aware of negative events such as racist encounters.

Take a moment to think about Melanie's and her parents' experience, and then respond to the questions below. This is an opportunity for you to think about how Melanie was affected. This could be helpful for you when monitoring your child's response to racial discrimination.

How did the coach's behavior cause Melanie to quit the cheerleading squad?

_____

_____

_____

Write down any signs of racial stress that Melanie showed.

_____

_____

_____

What do you think about how Melanie's parents handled the situation?

_____

_____

How would you have responded?

_____

_____

_____

_____

_____

_____

Every Child Is Unique

While racism can be harmful to kids, each kid responds differently to racial discrimination. As you read the next section, it is extremely important to keep in mind that sometimes kids can be okay. In other cases, they may be emotionally distressed. Fostering resilience can help prevent some of the detrimental effects of racism on children, but even resilient children may have emotional reactions to witnessing or experiencing racial discrimination.

One of the major factors that contribute to the emotional reaction of children to racism is how they perceive the event and internalize the experience. If two children witness racial discrimination, one child may adjust after the incident and not experience distress, and the other child may show significant emotional or behavioral symptoms.

As you continue through this workbook, it will be helpful to monitor your child to get a sense about how racism affects them. To do this, you can ask yourself: following racist incidents, are they having difficulties with being angry, focusing on schoolwork, or sleeping at night? If you notice difficulties, your child may not be adjusting well. In addition to monitoring your child, providing a supportive environment and helping them maintain a routine can help them be resilient. We will explore more strategies in chapters 3 to 5.

Remember that each child is different and unique. If you've previously talked with your child about racism, they may adjust without many difficulties.

Checking In with Your Child

When your child is having a hard time emotionally, you might notice that they avoid talking with you or they become consumed with solo activities, such as playing a video game or watching TV. It can be helpful to understand the differences between your child's typical emotional state and when they become stressed. Common signs of stress in children may include crying more than usual, not enjoying activities that used to be fun, acting irritable or angry, expressing fear, being clingy or not wanting to be out of your sight, or eating too much or too little.

You know your child better than anyone, and the questions that follow can help you understand whether they are experiencing stress.

What are some signs that your child is struggling?

_____

_____

_____

What do you typically do when you notice these signs?

_____

_____

_____

_____

What seems to help your child reduce stress?

_____

_____

_____

Who do you encourage your child to go to for support?

_____

_____

_____

_____

_____

_____

Checking in with your child regularly can help you with improving good communication and increase your awareness about things that lead to negative emotions. When you check in consistently with your child, you also help foster open communication, which makes it easier to talk about hard things as they become a teen—or even an adult. While it can be good to check in every day, that might not be easy, depending on your life. Try to check in as often as possible. If that means that you can only have a weekly check-in, that's okay. It might also be a good time to check in when you know of racial tension that is occurring in your community or society. A check-in can also be just observing your child's behavior or mood. That might be more manageable for your family, rather than having a sit-down discussion about their day. You can also use this rating scale to help you monitor your child throughout the week.

Child Symptoms Rating Scale

Rate each symptom on a scale from 0 to 2, where 0 = not at all, 1 = moderately, and 2 = extremely.

Day and date: _____

My child appears or feels:

Angry	0	1	2
Sad	0	1	2
Lonely	0	1	2
Worried	0	1	2
Scared	0	1	2
Clingy	0	1	2
Disappointed	0	1	2
Irritable or moody	0	1	2

If your child scores a 2 on any of these questions, it will be helpful to continue monitoring them over the next few days or weeks. If things don't improve, you may want to use the resources at the end of this workbook to find a mental health professional who can help you and your child cope with their difficulties.

Starting a Check-In Conversation

Sometimes children may hide how they feel or they may not verbally communicate it to you unless you initiate the conversation. I encourage you to take some time throughout the week to engage in conversations with your child to monitor their emotions and mental health. I know that life can be busy, and sometimes you may find it difficult to set aside a lot of time to talk with your child. However, these conversations don't have to be a formal sit-down meeting to talk about their day. You can initiate these invaluable conversations on car rides, while taking a walk, or when you sit down for dinner as a family. Having these conversations this way helps remove the pressure that comes with face-to-face conversations and helps the child feel more at ease to open up to you. Here are a few conversion starters that I encourage you to try using with your child.

- What happened today while you were at school?

- You look (happy, sad, angry, stressed) today. What's making you feel this way?

- Tell me one thing that brought you joy today.

- Tell me one thing that made you feel (happy, sad, angry, stressed) today.

- Sometimes kids are afraid to tell their parents how they feel. Have you ever felt like you couldn't tell me something? What made you feel that way?

Conversation Check-In Log

Over the next week, pick a different question to try each day (or come up with your own). After each conversation, use this log to reflect on the conversation. How did it go? Was your child open and responsive? Did some questions work better than others? What did you learn about your child that you didn't know before the conversation?

Day 1: _____

Question: _____

_____

_____

Reflection: _____

_____

_____

Day 2: _____

Question: _____

_____

_____

Reflection: _____

_____

_____

Day 3: _____

Question: _____

_____

_____

Reflection: _____

_____

_____

Day 4: _____

Question: _____

_____

_____

Reflection: _____

_____

_____

Day 5: _____

Question: _____

_____

_____

Reflection: _____

_____

_____

Day 6: _____

Question: _____

_____

_____

Reflection: _____

_____

_____

Day 7: _____

Question: _____

_____

_____

Reflection: _____

_____

_____

Let's return to the situation with Melanie. If her parents had taken some time to check in, they may have become aware of the incident with the coach. If Melanie were my child, I would have completed the rating scale and sat with her when I noticed that she was no longer excited about going to cheer practice. We would have discussed why she appeared to seem sad. This would have created an opportunity to support Melanie in the situation and address the racist comment made by the coach. If Melanie still did not want to continue cheerleading, we could have found another activity that she liked doing—particularly an activity where she could show up as her authentic self—so that she would not internalize the negative comment made by her coach.

Taking Care of Yourself Too

It is normal for your emotions to vary as you think about racism and begin to work through the exercises in this book. At times, you may feel that the work is draining your emotional energy. At times, you may feel hopeful that these strategies will be useful. I encourage you to be optimistic about your efforts and to keep in mind that healing *is* possible.

I occasionally feel these same emotions when I give a talk in the community on racial discrimination. What helps me continue to do this work is that I recognize that in the end it will be worth it. I urge you to continue pushing through these feelings, whether good or bad. Make sure that you take the time you need to slowly work through these exercises and activities. If you find it difficult the first time you work through an activity, give yourself permission to take a break. You can pause for a day and come back to the activity later. Keep in mind that change doesn't happen overnight. I often remind people who are starting therapy for the first time that progress takes time. The same thing is true for using this book as a tool to help your child. It will take time for you and your child to be comfortable processing racism. Over time, it will become easier to have these conversations with your child.

As you stay tuned in to your child's emotions, remember to stay tuned in to your own. Understanding your own emotions and how you cope is an important part of helping your child and fostering resilience. If you encounter situations that you can't seem to work through alone, consider seeking out a psychologist or therapist to help you. Remember that we can all benefit from therapy. It doesn't have to be the case that you seek therapy only because you have a mental health diagnosis or feel that life is extremely difficult. Therapy can be beneficial for you—as well as your child—in processing events such as racial discrimination or problem-solving situations you are experiencing as a family.

Time to Reflect

Using your journal or the space below, respond to these questions to reflect on your experience with this chapter.

Describe any symptoms of racial stress you've observed in your child. These symptoms may be emotional, behavioral, cognitive, or social.

_____

_____

_____

_____

Describe any symptoms you've noticed in yourself.

_____

_____

_____

_____

If you've talked with your child about racism or discrimination, what emotions did you notice in them?

_____

_____

What emotions did you feel?

_____

_____

Write down one or two things that helped you and your child cope with discomfort completing the activities in this chapter.

_____

_____

_____

_____

_____

_____

_____

Next Steps

So far we have explored in depth how racism and discrimination impact you and your child. Chapter 2 will help you prepare to engage in healthy conversations about racism. Your child may see how you cope with stress, and they may model those same healthy or unhealthy coping strategies, so one early step is being able to manage your own emotions and mental health. In the next chapter, we will explore the importance of self-care and identify what coping strategies are most helpful for you.

Managing Your Mental Health

Kids learn a lot from their environment and from you as their parent. Research has repeatedly shown that how we cope with stress models ways for our children to manage their own feelings, so to help your child cope with racial stress and thrive in society, one important step is recognizing how you navigate your own emotions around racial discrimination.

As you read earlier in this workbook, how you cope with racism will shape how you talk with your child about this topic. Using your life experiences and your own racial identity to talk with your child about racism will allow you to identify some healthy ways to help your child.

Parents are often concerned that having the race talk can make their child feel more negative about society, but in reality, *not* talking about it can lead them to internalize those negative messages about their race. They can end up blaming themselves for situations they had no control over, so it is critical that you allow yourself to get to a place where you're in an emotional state to have this difficult conversation. Processing these experiences for yourself will also help you learn how to cope with racial stress and allow you the opportunity to be honest with your emotions before engaging in these critical conversations with your child.

In this chapter, you will

- learn how racism impacts your own mental health and well-being;

- explore ways to manage your mental health by practicing self-compassion and self-care; and

- practice how to effectively model healthy coping skills to help your child thrive.

As you begin this chapter, I want you to recognize how important it is to take care of your own needs. A lot of the parents I work with typically prioritize the needs of their child, often to the detriment of their own mental health.

This observation is not an attack on anyone's parenting, including yours. Parenting is a big responsibility, and your child's needs are important. However, I want to encourage you to recognize that in order to take care of your child's needs you also need to be mentally healthy. You may have heard people say that "you can't pour from an empty cup," and that is particularly relevant when it comes to helping your child cope with racial discrimination.

Can you imagine trying to talk with your child about racism when you are extremely frustrated or hurt or emotionally drained? You may not be able to get your thoughts together. You may also be more likely to poorly manage your own emotions and break down crying. While there is nothing wrong with having an emotional breakdown, it would not be good to try talking with your child about racism at the same time.

In a perfect world, you wouldn't have to talk with your child about racism—but we all know that a perfect world doesn't exist so we must use each day to make our lives better. You have already demonstrated some resilience by working to overcome your own experiences with racism in society. Some of you have witnessed how your own parent(s) navigated these challenging situations, and this has given you motivation to push forward.

I know I'm preaching to the choir, but as you reflect throughout this chapter, and beyond, it is helpful to understand the psychological impacts of racism on *your* mental health. Decades of research have shown that racism and discrimination have many negative consequences for Black Americans (Pieterse et al. 2012). Racism can include individual, institutional, and cultural aspects (Jones 1997). At the individual level, racism happens when someone's bias or prejudiced attitudes result in their negatively judging another person. You may have experienced this when your child's teacher decided that they should not be in the gifted and talented program at school without even testing them for eligibility.

Racism at the institutional level can occur when individuals receive unfair or different access to goods and services, such as educational opportunities, fair housing, employment opportunities, or adequate medical care. Some parents may experience institutional racism when trying to vote in their community; for example, they may be required to provide additional forms of identification, which could impact their ability to contribute to the political process, preventing them from electing officials who may work to bring needed resources to their child's school or community.

Finally, cultural racialism occurs when white or European Americans' worldview and existence is valued within society more than those who are historically minoritized and marginalized (Jones 1997).

Your Experiences of Racism

Using the chart below, take a moment to reflect on your experiences of racism. Describe what happened, the type of racism you experienced (individual, institutional, or cultural), and how you reacted.

What Happened	Type of Racism	Your Reaction

Racism is a common occurrence, and taking care of yourself is an important way to be prepared. Examples of recent incidents of racial violence include the 2020 killing of George Floyd by a Minneapolis police officer and the 2023 shooting of Ajike "AJ" Owens by her neighbor. This devaluing of Black lives in American society can leave many of us saddened, hurt, angered, worried, or even depressed. As a parent, it can not only make you fear for your own life but obviously can make you concerned about your child's safety.

Experiencing or witnessing these types of racial incidents is associated with increased emotional difficulties and the risk of developing disorders such as post-traumatic stress disorder, commonly referred to as PTSD (Turner and Turner 2021). Racism in society as a whole and specifically in the workplace may cause stress, anxiety or depressive symptoms. After witnessing or experiencing discrimination you may have felt self-doubt, lowered expectations, or a sense of rejection. While Black men and women may have similar experiences due to their race, Black women may also experience discrimination due to their gender, putting them at higher risk of stress (Turner and Turner 2021).

• *The Case of Sheila*

Sheila is a twenty-eight-year-old African American woman who lives with her fiancé and their seven-year-old son. Recently, she was on social media after work and came across a disturbing post depicting racial violence toward a Black teen by his teacher at school. While her son had never experienced racial discrimination at school, and the family had a good relationship with the school staff, this post was unsettling.

Because of the violence she had witnessed on social media, she was more fearful about something happening to her son. To process the incident, Sheila talked with her fiancé about the video later that night. Their discussion left her feeling sad for a few days. She took some time for herself to manage her feelings and decide on a plan of action to make sure her son would be safe at school.

Later that week, Sheila decided that she would visit her son's school to see how the teachers generally behaved toward students. Her fears were lessened after observing how the teachers interacted with the students.

Sheila's story is one example of how racism can have an effect on your mental health. Not only did witnessing the racism increase Sheila's anxiety and sadness, it also changed her behavior; for example, she became more on alert about racial threats. Witnessing racism in your community or on social media can have a negative impact on your mental health, even if you don't experience it directly.

Take a moment to think about on Sheila's experience. If you experienced this situation, how do you think it would affect your mental health?

_____

_____

Who could you talk with about the situation; for example, a friend, family member, or partner?

_____

_____

What types of experiences have you observed on social media or in the news that triggered negative emotions or raised concerns about your child?

_____

_____

_____

How did you respond?

_____

_____

_____

_____

Racism and Your Mental Health

One area of concern that may impact your mental health is the fact that many Black children are targets of daily racial discrimination. According to an article published by the *Journal of Family Issues*, Black children are more likely to be seen as less innocent than their white peers, more likely to become victims of police brutality, and more likely to be suspended from school (Miller and Vittrup 2020). Knowing this information, it is possible that you may experience stress or anxiety about the safety of your child. I have encountered many parents who have expressed fear and anger about sending their child outside their home. Some parents worry about their child visiting a friend around the corner or attending school in a predominately white school district, where there is limited diversity in the school staff or among the students.

If you can identify with this situation, I encourage you to monitor your emotions and thoughts when you see racism occurring either in real life or on social media. It may also be helpful to take an inventory of your environment to get an idea about how safe or threatening the space may be for your family. When taking this inventory, it would be important to consider what you or your child worry about, such as the racial climate at school. For some parents, it may be the amount of over-policing in the community. Having a sense of this information can help you identify what would be important self-care practices to manage your mental health.

Although experiencing racism can be difficult, even processing or talking about these situations can be emotionally draining. You can probably recall a time in your own life when you either experienced or witnessed discrimination in society. Afterward, you may have felt depleted or emotionally drained. Sometime after I give a talk to other therapists about the psychological impacts of racism, or even when I teach students who are studying to be therapists, I have to allow myself time to emotionally recover.

An article published in the *Journal of Counseling Psychology* noted that perceived racial discrimination has a negative impact on mental health among Black Americans (Pieterse et al. 2012). The authors of the article found that, on average, Black Americans report higher exposure to racial discrimination compared to other groups. They also noted that this perceived discrimination was linked to higher levels of psychological distress and associated with reporting more mental health difficulties. In general, the data showed that experiencing and perceiving racism can lead to more negative emotions for parents, such as increased feelings of anxiety and depression.

Take a moment to think about how your experiences with racism have impacted you emotionally, and then write down your responses to these questions. Your experiences can be helpful to process with a therapist if you decide to go to therapy.

Describe a recent racist incident that you witnessed or experienced.

_____

_____

_____

_____

_____

How did it make you feel?

_____

_____

Write down any changes in your mood or behavior that you noticed following the incident.

_____

_____

If this incident brought up any fears or concerns about your child, what did you do to help you feel better?

_____

_____

_____

The Importance of Self-Care

Self-care can be defined as taking the time to do things that help you live well and improve both your physical health and mental health. The idea of practicing self-care is very trendy in today's society. You have probably seen social media posts related to self-care or had conversations with your friends about practicing self-care.

Obviously, self-care is a very broad term and can mean many different things for different people. Some of the common types of self-care that I discuss with parents include exercising, eating healthy, regularly drinking water, being outside in nature, sleeping, engaging in a relaxing activity such as journaling, and spending time with friends and family. My list may seem a bit obvious, but I think it is important to recognize that practicing self-care does not necessarily mean you need to spend a lot of money for activities like shopping, traveling, or eating a fancy meal. On the other hand, if you want to treat yourself to a trip to your favorite city or country from time to time, that can also be a nice self-care activity. What I often encourage people to understand is that self-care activities are ones you can do fairly often and on a consistent basis to help you manage and reduce your stress. While traveling or spending a lot of money are ways to practice self-care, they may not be ideal—or even possible—for everyone to do on a weekly basis.

In popular culture, we often think about self-care as physical (for example, exercise and healthy eating), social (for example, connecting with friends and family), or emotional (for example, using healthy coping strategies). In *The Self-Care Prescription*, psychologist Robyn Gobin (2019) expands this idea, describing self-care as consisting of six dimensions of wellness that can be helpful: physical, social, intellectual, vocational, spiritual, and emotional.

Some people may neglect dimensions that are less commonly thought of but can also be very helpful, such as spiritual, vocational, or intellectual self-care. Black culture often emphasizes the significance of spiritual practices; for centuries, spirituality has been an integral part of helping many Black families cope with racial injustice. For many of you, the belief in a higher power or God may play a significant role in your spiritual wellness.

I encourage you to identity your own self-care wellness plan, which may include at least one of these six self-care dimensions throughout your weekly routine.

Physical: Going for a walk or run, lifting weights, eating healthy, drinking adequate amounts of water, and getting eight hours of sleep

Social: Spending time with family or friends, having a game night with your kids, calling or video chatting with a friend, attending a support group

Intellectual: Doing a creative activity or hobby, reading a book, writing in a journal, listening to a podcast

Vocational: Identifying meaning in your work or vocation, using mindfulness or breathing exercises to prevent work burnout

Spiritual: Connecting with your religious or spiritual community, volunteering at your church, reading the Bible, praying, or connecting with a higher power by spending time in nature

Emotional: Using positive coping strategies such as meditation, journaling, listening to calming music, and maintaining healthy boundaries

This plan will be key to helping you emotionally prepare to talk with your child about the difficulties of navigating racial discrimination. Having a plan in advance will also make it easier to engage in the activity so that you don't have to problem solve in the moment. You will be prepared if things become emotionally charged.

Take some time to create your weekly self-care plan. Using the suggestions you just read, select at least one self-care practice that you can fit in your schedule. Consider adding details that would help make it easy to complete each week, such as the time of day, location of activity, or whether you will do the activity alone. For example, if you know that after work is the best time of day, you should write that down as part of your plan. Return to this worksheet as often as possible to revise your plan and reflect on how it helped your mood.

Self-Care Activity Schedule

Day	Plan for Self-Care Activity
Monday	
Tuesday	
Wednesday	
Thursday	
Friday	
Saturday	
Sunday	

Strategies to Manage Your Mental Health

In addition to self-care, there are many other ways to manage your mental health following experiences of racial discrimination of any type: individual, institutional, or cultural. It is important to not only have an awareness of how you are being impacted by racism but also to figure out the best way to cope. Not taking care of yourself can lead to negative consequences, such as more stress, poor parenting, and even chronic health issues. It's also important to take care of yourself because it's necessary to help your child manage their own mental health and emotions. This is especially important as you prepare to have the race talk.

I recognize that your priorities are likely to shift once you have children. Most of the time, your needs may become secondary to caring for your child. Trying to help another human being cope with a situation is never easy when you are overwhelmed or stressed out. For example, think back to a time in your life when you had a really long, difficult day at work and headed home with the expectation that you would need to help your child with a difficult homework assignment. How did that situation go? More than likely you found yourself with a low frustration tolerance or maybe even had difficulty understanding the task that needed to be completed because your brain could not think clearly.

The same thing can happen when you are trying to talk with your child effectively about managing their emotional reaction to racial discrimination. My advice to you as you continue working through this book is that you remember that you are human and also deserve care and compassion.

The idea of caring for yourself and being kind to yourself is nothing new. However, I think that after living through a pandemic and a racial reckoning, many of us have begun to realize that we all need to give ourselves more grace. As a parent, you may feel pressure to always do things "perfectly" and to raise a "perfect" child, but the reality is that there is no such thing as perfection. As I tell my clients all the time, raising a child doesn't come with a manual. Most parents either learn how to parent along the way, or they build on what they witnessed from their own parents and viewed as being helpful or good. If they didn't find certain things helpful, they most often try to avoid repeating those patterns.

You have probably made some decisions that you look back on and think that you could have done something differently. That's perfectly okay. Life is about growth. My hope is this workbook creates space for you to grow in your approaches to help your child be more resilient when facing racial discrimination. It is also important to recognize that how you take care of your own emotions can play a critical role in how your child copes with similar negative experiences such as racial stress. So as you prepare to help them, you must first learn to take care of your mental health needs.

Using CBT Strategies to Cope

As you read earlier, CBT is a psychological approach that focuses on the connections between your thoughts, emotions, and behaviors. CBT strategies can help address a variety of problems, including anxiety, depression, low self-esteem, anger, and other emotional difficulties. One of the primary aspects of CBT is helping people understand how their thoughts about situations can lead to positive and negative emotions. For example, viewing an incident of racial discrimination can lead someone to feel anxiety about interacting with people that identify as non-Black.

There can be many reasons for experiencing this kind of anxiety or racial stress. One trigger may be when someone has thoughts about how they may be treated by a white person. Think back to Sheila's story; her thoughts about her son experiencing unfair treatment at school due to his race caused her to be worried and concerned about his safety. To reduce her anxiety, she made a decision to take action and visit the school. In her case, being reassured eased her fears and worries. I hope that you are able to work through the CBT strategies below to help you cope and being to model healthy ways that can help your child thrive.

CBT strategies work by helping you learn to identify how situations or thoughts trigger negative emotions and how those triggers influence your emotions and behavior.

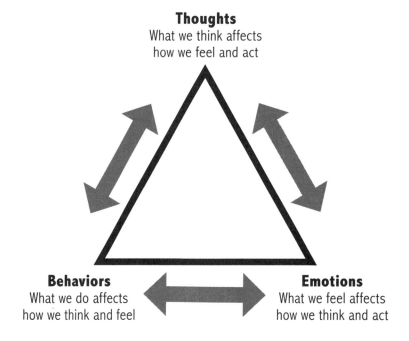

CBT triangle

Thinking about certain situations can bring up automatic negative emotions, like anxiety, or cause you to cope with the situation by behaving in particular way. For example, if you have been stopped by a police officer when you were not breaking any law, that experience may have led to fear or anger, which are appropriate emotions in that circumstance. You may have been stopped by the police when "driving while Black." Personally, when I have been pulled over on a highway for no evident reason, my body becomes tense, and my anxiety soars. I wonder if I have been targeted. I worry that I could be shot. Unfortunately, the reality is that over the years, we have seen far too many Black people shot and killed by police when they were abiding by the law and did not have any weapons, or even were just sleeping in their homes. Given what we know, it is realistic to have some anxiety about interactions with police officers. To reduce the stress from these interactions, it is helpful to avoid blaming yourself and having thoughts like *I should have just avoided this neighborhood* or *I could have spoken in a calm voice*. While there may have been little you could do in this type of situation, CBT strategies can help avoid thinking errors that lead to more negative emotions.

Some of the most helpful CBT techniques include the following:

- identifying your triggers

- keeping track of your thinking patterns

- recording your emotional responses to triggers

- practicing ways to respond in different situations

In order to help your child cope with racial stress, it will be important for you to learn more about managing the situations that trigger your anger, worry, or sadness. Working to understand yourself and identify your own emotions, thoughts, and behaviors can make it easier to help your child with identifying their experiences. The questions that follow provide a chance for you to reflect on your past experiences with racism, explore your automatic thoughts and emotions, and process your actions.

Describe a past situation where you experienced racism or perceived discrimination. Where did it happen? Who was present? What happened?

_____

_____

_____

_____

_____

What thoughts popped up in your head during the situation?

_____

_____

What emotions did you experience? Were you angry, hurt, worried, shocked, or numb?

_____

_____

What did you do to cope? Did you talk to a friend or family member? Did you isolate yourself? Did you engage in an unhealthy coping mechanism, such as having a drink?

_____

_____

_____

_____

Now it's time to think about some strategies to help process those experiences and learn additional ways to cope in the future. Keep in mind that these strategies will not only be helpful for you but they will also be great to model healthy coping for your child. The next few pages will offer some CBT strategies you can use for coping with racial stressors.

Identifying and Coping with Your Triggers

Triggers are people, places, words, things, or thoughts that lead to undesired emotions or responses. Keep in mind that different situations may activate different types of triggers. The activity that follows will help you identify your racial triggers and learn strategies to cope in the moment.

Describe a recent situation where you were triggered by witnessing racial discrimination.

_____

_____

_____

_____

_____

_____

_____

_____

_____

What triggered you in this situation?

_____

_____

_____

Think about what generally triggers you and describe it here:

People _____

_____

_____

_____

Places _____

_____

_____

Words _____

_____

_____

Things _____

_____

_____

_____

Thoughts _____

_____

_____

_____

_____

_____

There are many ways to cope with triggers, including

removing yourself from the situation (if possible);

minimizing exposure to triggers;

counting down from 10 to 0;

calmly stating what you need in that moment; and

discussing the situation with a trusted friend.

What do you think would help you best cope with your triggers?

_____

_____

_____

_____

_____

_____

Deep Breathing

Anger and anxiety are common emotions that many people experience when they encounter racial discrimination. Both are healthy human emotions, although we might sometimes express these emotions in an unhealthy way. Unhealthy anger may show up as physical or verbal aggression. Anxiety may be experienced as muscle tension, sweaty hands, an increased heart rate, or difficulty breathing.

This simple breathing exercise can help you de-escalate these intense emotions. It is helpful to practice several times before trying to use this exercise in a situation when you are triggered.

Find a quiet place where you won't be interrupted.

Get into a comfortable position. You may want to sit in a chair with your feet flat on the floor, sit on the floor with your back against a wall, or lie down.

Close your eyes if you choose.

Slowly breathe in through your nose and fill your stomach with air. You should feel a slight tightness in your diaphragm (the area below the center of your chest).

Hold the air for about five seconds and then slowly breathe out through your mouth.

Repeat this pattern of breathing ten to fifteen times, or until you feel relaxed.

Once you have learned to use this breathing exercise, you can use the strategy in situations where you feel triggered.

Activities to Help You Cope

Below is a list of things you can consider doing to help you manage your emotions when you experience stress related to racism. Put a check next to those you think would best work in your situation.

☐ Read your favorite book or magazine.

☐ Listen to a podcast or music.

☐ Watch a television show or stream a movie.

☐ Take a walk.

☐ Do some exercise.

☐ Make time to relax with your friends or family.

☐ Talk to a trusted friend or ally.

☐ Connect with a community or religious organization.

☐ Journal or write positive affirmations.

Write down other things you find helpful: _____

_____

_____

_____

As you continue in this workbook, you'll find more examples and exercises to help you and your child. I encourage you to begin practicing these strategies in your daily life. This practice will make it easier for you to model these skills for your child and work through similar activities with them. As you get more comfortable using the skills, you can slowly introduce them to your child.

• *The Case of Jason*

Jason is a thirty-six-year-old African American male who is co-parenting with his ex-wife. They have both remarried but maintain a good relationship for the sake of raising their ten-year-old daughter. When Jason was at the mall with his daughter to buy a Christmas gift, a buzzer went off as they were leaving the store. They were stopped by a white security guard, who immediately pushed Jason against the wall and yelled at him while his daughter stood by crying in fear.

When the store cashier ran over to intervene, the security guard realized that the cashier had forgotten to remove the security tag from the merchandise, and he let Jason and his daughter leave the store. As they walked away, the security guard yelled after them, "If Black people stopped stealing from here, this wouldn't have happened."

After they got home, Jason told his ex-wife what had happened. They were both upset about the incident, but Jason decided to not talk with his daughter because he was at a loss for what to say. Now every time Jason wants to take his daughter to the mall she begs to stay home with her mother.

In this scenario, Jason and his daughter were rightfully upset following the incident at the mall. While it's hard to say what Jason was thinking, his daughter was clearly fearful. This fear resulted in her changing her behavior and not wanting to go to the mall anymore.

As you read earlier, one way that children learn is through observing. What may have helped in this scenario is for Jason to have first processed his own feelings, identified some coping strategies (such as deep breathing), and then talked with his daughter about those feelings to normalize her feelings about the situation. Because his daughter was unable to observe how Jason used healthy coping following the incident, she was stuck not knowing how she should cope herself.

I encourage you to make a mental note to return to this section as needed to work through your own situations. This review will help you better prepare to model healthy coping for your child. As the saying goes, practice makes perfect. So the best way to learn how to identify and use healthy coping strategies is to practice as often as possible. Generally, I ask my clients to practice skills weekly. Since you are working through these skills in your home, you will need to identify your own practice plan. Having these tools at hand can be a useful resource when it's time to help your child cope with racial discrimination.

Take a moment to reflect on Jason's experience with his daughter.

What are your thoughts about the scenario?

_____

_____

_____

_____

_____

_____

How might you apply some of the strategies discussed earlier in the chapter?

_____

_____

_____

_____

_____

What do you think about his decision to not talk with his daughter about the incident?

_____

_____

How do you think you would have handled the situation if this happened to you and your child?

_____

_____

_____

What advice would you give Jason to cope in the situation or to prepare his child?

_____

_____

_____

_____

Modeling Healthy Coping

When you tell kids how to behave in situations and you behave differently, they'll typically imitate what you did as opposed to what you told them to do. I often talk with parents about the power of observational learning; that is, learning by example. Observational learning is a concept that was demonstrated by psychologist Albert Bandura. In his work, Bandura described the ways in which children learn by watching the actions of other trusted people (Bandura, Grusec, and Menlove 1966). As you begin to give your child tools and strategies to manage their emotions, keep in mind the importance of modeling healthy ways of coping through your actions.

Ask Dr. Earl

A parent asks...

My favorite self-care practice is doing a walking meditation. I go for a walk to clear my mind. I have tried to get my child to go with me because I know that walking helps me with my stress. However, every time I ask her to join me she doesn't even want to try it. How can I model healthy self-care practices when she doesn't want to learn?

And I answer...

Kudos to you for having a self-care routine and encouraging your child to develop a routine by modeling this behavior. While modeling can often lead to your child engaging in the same behavior to cope, they may engage in the activity with you and still decide to not use the self-care practice in their daily life. It's important to remember that, while modeling is helpful for teaching your child coping skills, you also need to maintain *your* mental health. Using healthy self-care strategies will allow you to improve your well-being. If your child is having difficulties engaging, it may be helpful to find out what types of things she enjoys and then you both can try that self-care activity together. Creating a list of options is also a good idea, so you can use a different strategy when you're unable to engage in your usual self-care practice. This routine can be helpful for your child as she learns and grows.

Time to Reflect

Using your journal or the space below, respond to these questions to reflect on your experience with this chapter.

What is your current self-care routine?

_____

_____

_____

_____

_____

What self-care activities do you find most useful?

_____

_____

_____

Have you been able to practice the CBT strategies? If not, what prevented you from practicing?

_____

_____

_____

_____

What strategies did you find easy or challenging?

_____

_____

_____

_____

Write down one or two things that you plan to continue practicing and modeling to help your child cope with racial discrimination.

_____

_____

_____

_____

_____

_____

_____

Next Steps

At this point you have learned the importance of managing your own mental health and the benefits of having a self-care routine. It's important to identify self-care practices that you can use often to help reduce stress and improve your well-being, such as deep breathing. In chapter 3, we will begin to explore the importance of having healthy conversations about race and strategies for supporting positive racial identity.

Increasing Resilience with Racial Socialization

One way to reduce the impact of racism on your child and promote emotional well-being is by proactively engaging in racial socialization; that is, teaching them what it means to be Black or African American. The primary goals of racial socialization are to help them talk about racial encounters, prepare them for emotional reactions, and reduce racial stress and trauma after they have experienced racial discrimination.

Beginning in early childhood, parents can engage in intentional conversations with children, instilling pride about their race and culture, and preparing them to deal with discrimination in society.

In this chapter, you will

- gain a better understanding of the importance of talking with children about their race and racial identity;

- learn how to create an environment to support emotional well-being among children who have experienced indirect or direct exposure to racism; and

- begin to use strategies to engage in the race talk and to engage in healthy conversations with your child to help them cope with racism.

What Is Racial Socialization?

Racial socialization has been described as an approach that emphasizes both verbal and nonverbal communications between a parent and their child about the importance of race, interacting with people from different racial groups, and awareness of the positive aspects of one's racial identity (Jones and Neblett 2017; Stevenson and Arrington 2009). For example, some parents may teach their kids to not touch toys in the store for fear that the clerk may see them, follow them around the store, and accuse them of stealing. These types of situations may happen without their conscious awareness, but the messages are often intended to protect your child from further racial harassment. Preparing your child to deal with bias and discrimination is only one part of the socialization process. Racial socialization focuses on communicating cultural knowledge, cultural practice, and history (Hughes et al. 2006). Regardless of where you live and your economic background, Black children continue to be at a higher risk of experiencing discrimination and racism compared to their non-Black peers. Therefore, it is necessary that you have the tools to engage in racial socialization with your child. It is important to have a healthy balance of preparing your child to experience racial discrimination and to have pride in their identity.

How Racial Socialization Promotes Coping and Resilience

Talking with children about their racial identity and how to cope with racial bias helps reduce their stress and promotes positive self-esteem. Why? The answer is complex. Having the race talk with your child helps promote resilience and prevents your child from internalizing negative messages about themselves and their identity. Engaging in racial socialization allows you to highlight positive aspects of your child's identity and your culture, as opposed to focusing only on problems like racial discrimination. For example, parents may prepare their child to experience bias—such as having a teacher who perceives them as not being smart enough to complete an exceptional science project by themselves—without countering that message by sharing with children that many Black people have made great contributions to society, such as Garrett Morgan Sr., who invented the traffic light. When you engage in racial socialization, you help your child avoid believing messages from society that they're not good enough and also emotionally recover from racist encounters.

Child development experts note that children cannot be understood outside of their context; development should be understood within the transactional relationship between children and their social and physical environments (Grills et al. 2016). What this means is that the community your child lives in—including factors within the home, school, and other areas of the child's life—influences their psychological and emotional development. Racial socialization takes into account your child's environment and experiences to prepare them to be resilient to racism. For example, worrying about racism that occurred in the community can cause children to have problems at school. Due to their stress or worries, your child may have difficulties focusing on completing schoolwork. Therefore, it's important to engage in racial socialization to improve your child's overall development.

Ask Dr. Earl

A parent asks...

I hear lots of people talking about racial socialization, but I'm nervous about starting the race talk with my child. How can I talk about racial differences? What is a good age to start doing this with my child?

And I answer...

There is a lot of research on the benefits of starting these conversations early with your child. Most children begin to recognize racial differences as early as age three. Children notice that their skin or hair may be different from their non-Black friends. It is helpful to have age-appropriate conversations and activities to talk about racial differences. To start this socialization, try reading books on skin color, going to museums to learn about historical events such as school segregation or voting rights, and using activism to speak out against negative racial stereotypes. During these activities, you can ask your child questions such as "What do you notice?"; "How does it make you feel?"; and "How have people been treated differently based on being Black?"

You'll find additional prompts for discussion later in this chapter.

Reflecting on Your Own Racial Socialization

As a parent, your responsibility is to raise your child so that they can develop a healthy sense of agency, belonging, competence, and power. Through engaging in racial socialization with your child, you can empower them to build traits necessary for positive development. If your child were upset about not understanding their homework, you would probably sit with them, talk through the assignment, and help them feel motivated to do the work. However, when children experience or witness racism, some parents will simply say, "It's not your fault," and try to move on from the situation. While that approach can help your child move past the negative experience in the moment, it doesn't help their self-esteem in the long run or teach them how to deal with the experience if it happens again. This can leave your child feeling like it's their fault, and they don't feel empowered to respond to the negativity.

Research indicates that the way parents talk with children about racism is often based on their own experiences (Jones and Neblett 2019). If you grew up in a home where there were no explicit conversations around confronting racism or preparing you to deal with discrimination, you may be less inclined to have direct conversations with your own children. However, if you have witnessed or experienced some type of racial discrimination, you have probably already considered the importance of preparing your child to experience bias or discrimination.

I understand that talking about, experiencing, and witnessing racism and discrimination can be psychologically painful for you as a parent, causing you to have fear about engaging in racial socialization with your child. I encourage you to move through this work at a pace that you feel comfortable with. If you run into some discomfort, allow yourself some grace, perhaps taking a few moments to engage in self-care or even taking a break for the day.

The questions that follow are meant to help you understand how your personal experiences with racism and discrimination have contributed to how you have engaged in racial socialization with your child. You can think about your own childhood or what you have done to this point with your child. This reflection will help you identify examples that will be useful as you work through this chapter. If you haven't engaged in racial socialization, that's okay. I hope that reflecting on your own experiences will give you some ideas about the best ways to have these types of conversations with your child.

At what age did you first learn about racism and discrimination?

_____

What has racial socialization looked like for you in the past?

_____

_____

_____

_____

What conversations did you have with your parents during your childhood about racism and discrimination?

_____

_____

_____

_____

How has this shaped your preparation to talk to your child?

_____

_____

How do you feel about talking with your child about navigating racism in society?

_____

_____

What makes you confident or fearful about having this talk?

_____

_____

_____

Describe any background that you believe would be useful to share with your child about their race and cultural heritage.

_____

_____

_____

_____

_____

_____

Every Black parent has had different experiences with racial socialization in their own childhood. It's natural that if you didn't have the race talk with your parents, you may not have considered having it with your child. However, in the current context of increased racial injustice and anti-Black racism, it may be helpful for you to do things differently than your parents did. This may include having more conversations about race, racial identity, and addressing racism in your community. From your personal experiences, you already have an awareness about how your childhood influenced the person you are today. For example, if you believed that your parents did a good job using discipline in your home when you were growing up, that belief probably led you to use similar parenting strategies with your child. However, if you didn't agree with those strategies that they used, you may have decided on a different approach to discipline your child.

• *The Case of Nicole*

Nicole is a thirty-one-year-old Black woman who lives in the northeastern part of the United States. She lives with her partner and their seven-year-old son. Nicole had a pretty unremarkable childhood. She is the middle of three children and was raised by both her parents. She recalls that when she was twelve one of her teachers called her by a racial slur. After the incident she told her parents, and they addressed the issue with the school. However, she never had a detailed conversation with her parents about that experience. Although she felt supported by her parents, she remembers experiencing a lot of ongoing uncertainty about returning to school, not knowing whether the incident would happen again or her peers would make similar comments to her.

Recently, Nicole heard about a school resource officer engaging in racial violence toward a student at her son's school. Her son was not aware of the incident because he was in class when it happened. Although the school principal and staff attempted to keep the violence hidden from most of the school, the incident made the local news. When Nicole and her partner watched the news coverage of the surveillance camera, they felt it was necessary to check in with their son and have the race talk. While they had not previously discussed racism with him, they felt this was a good time, given what had happened at his school.

In this case, Nicole recalled how she was impacted by racial discrimination as a child. Although her parents contacted her school to deal with the situation, she didn't process the experience with them. Given her experience, she recalled some discomfort and anxiety about going to school. As a result, Nicole and her partner made the decision to engage in racial socialization by preparing their child to deal with potential racial bias and discrimination. Although her son had not witnessed or experienced racism, they wanted to be proactive in case he learned about the racial violence at his school.

Being proactive is an important part of racial socialization. However, there is the possibility that some of these discussions will emotionally impact children. For example, Nicole's son may have some anxiety about going to school or fear about the same thing happening to him. To minimize your child's potential emotional discomfort, it can help to reassure them by discussing any plans you have made to keep them safe or letting them know that you have talked with their teacher or school staff to make sure it's okay for them to go to school. You can also refer back to chapter 1 about how to talk with children about racism. As you continue in this workbook, remember that each action you take to support your child will help them be resilient and thrive in the face of racism.

Before moving forward, take a few moments to reflect on Nicole's story.

How did Nicole's experience with racism in her childhood influence her decision to have the race talk with her child?

_____

_____

_____

_____

Would you make the same decision as Nicole did if it was your child? Why or why not?

_____

_____

_____

Before talking with their child about racism, how could Nicole and her partner take care of themselves? What coping skills should they prepare to model for their child?

_____

_____

_____

_____

_____

When Should Racial Socialization Start?

Although many parents may not consciously consider when to start racial socialization, the reality is that you may have already started the process without thinking about it. Often we learn about our racial background and negative perceptions about our racial identity at a very young age. These views are sometimes shared from generation to generation without there being a direct conversation about racial discrimination. In my experience, parents' attitudes and behaviors communicate their worldview about their race and ethnicity to their children in different ways: subtle or overt, deliberate or unintended. Sometimes it's not just what you say but also what your child observes. So the truth is by age three, your child has learned something about racial differences. This means that even when you don't verbally communicate messages about racial pride or devaluation of one's culture by society, your child may notice your actions, and that can influence how they think about themselves and their racial background.

Let's look at the ways you have already communicated about race to your child whether directly or indirectly.

First, what messages did you receive about race as you were growing up? These messages may have come from your parents or other people, such as teachers or coaches.

_____

_____

_____

_____

_____

How have you indirectly communicated the importance of being Black to your child? Have you responded to racism without saying anything to your child?

_____

_____

_____

Have you had direct conversations with your child about race or racism? Why or why not? What do you recall telling them?

_____

_____

_____

_____

_____

_____

These questions allowed you some space to consider how you may have unconsciously taken steps to engage in racial socialization. The rest of the chapter will offer some additional tools and reflection exercises to help with racial socialization.

Starting the Conversation

It's important to feel comfortable when starting conversations about race and racism with your child. You may worry about how to respond if your child asks you hard questions. My hope is that as you work your way through this book it will get easier to find the best approach for you and your child. I recommend that you start by trying to understand your own feelings and emotions. If your emotions are raw it may be difficult for you to engage in a productive discussion with your child. Anger, fear, or sadness are okay—but you should process those feelings before you talk with your child about racially motivated experiences. It can be less helpful to attempt to have a conversation with your child about race or racism in the heat of the moment.

The worksheet that follows can help you prepare for a conversation about race and identity with your child. This information will also be helpful as you proceed through the next few sections of the book. I recommend completing the worksheet in advance of a conversation and keeping it nearby when you talk with your child.

Before you begin, take a survey of your feelings. Where do you fall on a scale of 1 (totally calm) to 10 (extremely agitated)? If your score is 5 or higher, you may want to consider a better time to have the conversation. What would help you feel calmer?

_____

_____

_____

_____

If you have decided to continue, what are the key messages you want to communicate to your child? For example, do you want to talk with them about their racial identity?

_____

_____

_____

_____

_____

_____

_____

Activity: Racial Socialization Conversation Starters

Take a look at these conversation starters below and begin by answering them for yourself.

What do you know about people from different races?

_____

_____

_____

What does being Black mean to you?

_____

_____

Where did you learn that?

_____

_____

What makes you proud about being Black?

_____

_____

What makes you feel good about yourself?

_____

_____

It can be helpful to have an idea about how you could respond to your child if they don't have an answer to the prompt or if they ask you to respond to the same question.

What questions do you imagine your child asking in response? Do you feel ready to answer them?

_____

_____

_____

_____

_____

Promoting Cultural and Racial Pride

One aspect of racial socialization is *cultural socialization,* which involves messages and behaviors that emphasize having pride in one's race, culture, and heritage (Anderson et al. 2018). For Black youth, cultural socialization helps improve resilience by increasing positive racial identity. When you engage in discussions with your child about their race and identity, it helps them feel positive about who they are and increases their understanding about parts of their culture.

Reading is a good way to engage in cultural socialization and promote racial literacy. In the Resources section at the back of this book, you'll find a list of books you can use for those purposes. To help your child think about how race is important to their identity and to increase their self-esteem, try asking them questions about a specific character in the book; for example, "What do you notice about _____?" "How do you think _____ _____ feels?" "How does what happened to _____ make you feel"? You can then share with them more about your perspective.

The discussion prompts that follow can also be helpful in talking with your child when watching a movie or TV show, attending a museum exhibit about racism or social justice, or after exposing your child to activism.

- *Sometimes people are treated differently because they are Black. In this (movie/exhibit/TV show), what was one way you saw someone being treated unfairly or differently?*

- *Black people have made great achievements and contributions to society and our community. What have you learned at school about one famous Black civil rights hero? (You can then share Black history facts with your child. You'll find helpful sources in the Resources section)*

- *Tell me how you felt after this (movie/exhibit/TV show). What made you feel that way?*

- *Tell me what happened to the Black child (adult) in that TV show (movie). Why do you think that happened?*

- *What did you learn from this museum exhibit?*

- *What was one thing that made you feel happy to be Black?*

- Create your own prompt(s): _____

- _____

- _____

- _____

The worksheet that follows will give you some further guidance on exploring racial pride with your child. You can use it along with a book or movie that focuses on race and culture; see the Resources section for ideas. This is a chance for you to learn about your child and to help them think about how their race brings them joy and pride. Before completing this worksheet with your child, you may want to think through these prompts so that you can also share your own answers. If your child has a hard time sharing, you can share first to help them think about their responses.

Cultural and Racial Pride Worksheet

Using the space below, work with your child to identify positive aspects of their racial identity and culture.

What is something you like about yourself?

_____

_____

What is something you like about our family?

_____

_____

What is something in our culture that makes you feel proud to be Black?

_____

_____

Name one thing that you take pride in.

_____

Name one historical figure or famous Black person who makes you feel proud, and tell why you chose that person.

_____

_____

• *The Case of Jamal*

Jamal is a seven-year-old boy who lives with his parents and older sister. One day, he came home from school upset because the teacher had used a racial slur in talking to him and then said, "You're not smart like the other boys." He told his parents what had happened, and they were angry. Living in a diverse community, they had not experienced anything like this before. Jamal's parents decided to talk with him about the situation so they could better understand how it impacted his feelings and thoughts about the teacher and returning to school.

During the conversation, his parents learned that he was confused by the comment, worried about going back to school, and sad that the teacher had been mean. He told his parents that his teacher "is always mean to him and the other Black kids." His parents responded by comforting him, telling him that sometimes people make rude comments, and he was not responsible for the teacher's insensitive and biased behavior.

In this case, let's assume that Jamal and his parents identify the statement by the teacher as racial discrimination. To help Jamal better process the event, his parents could have attempted to promote positive racial socialization through highlighting his personal achievements and sharing experiences of other African Americans who have been academically successful. It is also important to recognize that having this conversation with Jamal helps prepare him in case he experiences racial bias or discrimination in society in the future.

This type of socialization can help protect your child from believing negative messages about their racial identity. Having healthy conversation about one's race helps reduce negative mental health outcomes such as anxiety, poor self-esteem, or depression.

Take a few moments to think about Jamal's case. Here are some reflection questions you can use to consider Jamal's experience and how you might respond as a parent.

How did Jamal's experience with racism at school influence his emotions, thoughts, and behavior?

_____

_____

_____

_____

Would you make the same decision as Jamal's parents? Why or why not?

_____

_____

_____

_____

_____

If you were Jamal's parent, what could you do to increase his cultural and racial pride?

_____

_____

_____

_____

_____

Using Positive Self-Talk to Grow Resilience

Teaching children to engage in *positive self-talk*—that is, repeating positive messages or affirmations to themselves—is one way to help them combat negative messages about their racial identity and improve their mood and self-esteem. Using positive self-talk with your child also allows you the opportunity to model coping and promote empowerment. Positive self-talk helps children modify their thoughts instead of allowing negative thoughts about their race to paralyze them, resulting in mental health difficulties, such as racial stress.

In Jamal's story, his teacher implied that he was not smart because of his race. As a result, he could have experienced negative thoughts about himself or found it hard to believe he could succeed in school. Instead of telling himself *I'm not a smart kid*, he would affirm his own ability to do well with a message such as *I can do well in school.*

Now that you have a better understanding about your child's experience with racism, you can begin to help them change negative self-talk by using positive self-talk or creating positive affirmations. The goal is to help your child following experiences of racial discrimination. You will need to guide your child through practicing positive self-talk to challenge negative messages about their identity. For example, a statement like "You're not good enough" can be combated by using positive self-talk such as "I can do as well as the other kids." With practice, this will become easier for your child to use. It can be helpful to create a list of positive self-statements for your child to practice throughout the week. The worksheet that follows will help you guide your child through using positive self-talk. You can work with your child on it as often as you feel helpful. To start, I suggest you set a goal to check in with your child at least once a week.

Creating Positive Self-Talk

Take a moment to identify a racist encounter with your child. You can refer back to the example you discussed before with your child, use one of the book suggestions in the Resources section, or find a new example (either from TV or your child's experience at school or in the community).

_____

_____

_____

_____

_____

_____

_____

Using the space that follows, write down your child's thoughts about what is going on in the example you identified. Before you share your own opinion, try to ask questions such as "What do you remember seeing or observing?" As they share, be supportive and validate their thoughts and feelings.

_____

_____

_____

_____

Once you review the encounter with your child, try to understand the types of negative messages or negative self-talk your child identifies from the example. If you're using an example from TV or a book, you could ask "Why do you think they were treated that way?" Make sure that you allow your child to use their own words. If you need to help them with vocabulary, use limited prompting. Write down the negative message here.

_____

_____

_____

_____

Using that information, now write down the negative self-talk statement. For example, Jamal's self-talk statement was "I'm not smart because I'm Black." You may have to work with your child to identify the negative self-talk. If the child doesn't verbalize a clear statement, that's okay. As long as you have a sense of the negative thought(s), you can work to create positive self-talk.

_____

_____

_____

Finally, take a moment to discuss the experience with your child. Work with your child to create some sample positive statements to use. Jamal's was "I can do well in school." Remind your child to try using a positive statement or affirmation each day. They can decide to either write the statement down, make a sign to put on the wall or refrigerator, or say the statement each day before going to school.

_____   _____

_____

_____

During the week, I encourage you to continue practicing positive self-talk or using positive affirmations with your child. You may not see the changes in your child right away, but over time you will be able to witness how practicing these skills helps them become more resilient. Here are some positive affirmations you can encourage your child to use:

- Being different makes me beautiful inside and out.

- I deserve love and kindness from everyone.

- I love my Black skin.

- Being Black is my superpower.

- I am smart and can be successful.

Fostering Empowerment and Change

Change doesn't happen overnight. If you go to therapy, you can't expect to have one session and get relief from your negative emotions. Similarly, it can take some time for your child to learn all the tools they need to thrive. You may notice that your child has a hard time doing these activities at first, and that is to be expected.

To help your child, be sure to encourage them to share. Let them know that there is no right or wrong way to respond. Empowering your child will be really important throughout this process. Be flexible with your child and try to stay motivated as you work on these skills. Setting a goal of practicing one skill each week can help you both with motivation. At the end of the week, you can reward your child with a treat or doing a fun activity together that they enjoy.

Time to Reflect

Using your journal or the space below, respond to these questions to reflect on your experience with this chapter.

Describe your experience working on racial socialization with your child.

_____

_____

_____

_____

_____

What was easy or difficult for you?

_____

_____

_____

What do you think was easy or difficult for your child?

_____

_____

_____

What helped you cope as you were working through the activities?

_____

_____

_____

Going forward, what would you consider doing for self-care?

_____

_____

_____

_____

_____

_____

_____

Next Steps

So far we have taken time to discuss how racism can cause stress and emotional difficulties in your child. In order to reduce possible stress, engaging in racial socialization is helpful to promote resilience. As you use the strategies and exercises in this chapter, remember that it is important to balance preparation for bias and fostering racial pride in your child. In the next chapter, we will begin to discuss how racial literacy and activism can also be used as a coping strategy.

CHAPTER 4

Helping Children Thrive Through Activism

In many oppressed and marginalized communities, activism and social justice efforts have always played a role. Engaging in activism helps facilitate change in the community and reduce discrimination. Historically, children of all ages have taken part in activism when they joined their parents at protests, rallies, or peaceful demonstrations.

Activism can be a helpful tool for helping your child cope with racial discrimination and thrive. It can help promote resilience and empower your child to think critically about the ways civic engagement can also help create change and fight oppressive systems. Engaging in activism with your child at an early age can help combat feelings of hopelessness they may be experiencing. When a child feels like there is no way to prevent people from making hurtful racist statements or treating them unfairly because of their race, they are more likely to experience racial stress.

In this chapter, you will

- gain an understanding of how activism can help foster community engagement and resilience;

- explore the types of activism and gain a better understanding of how activism can be a tool for coping with racial stress; and

- learn how to use activism as a teachable moment to increase racial socialization and resilience.

Assessing Your Starting Point

Before you engage in activism with your child, it can be helpful to identify where to begin. Part of the process of identifying your own starting point is exploring how you engaged in activism throughout your own childhood. You may have grown up in a family where your parents did work in the community, fighting for equity and racial justice. You may have had limited experience engaging in activism because your parents did not have the time or the desire, or perhaps they did not know how to start. Whatever the reason, you can now take a moment to think about the role of activism and how it may be useful for your family.

Using the questions below, take a moment to reflect on your experience with activism in your own childhood and how that experience contributes to your thinking about engaging in activism with your child. Remember, there are no right or wrong responses. This is an opportunity for you to better explore how it may be easier or more challenging to consider engaging in different types of activism as a family.

Describe your experience with activism in your childhood or adolescence. What did your parents teach you about activism? What social justice or civil rights movements did your parents teach you about; for example, how children worked to help desegregate schools?

_____

_____

_____

_____

_____

What have you told your child about activism? Have you taken your child with you to protest injustice in your community? Have you observed protests around the world through news media?

_____

_____

_____

At times, the thought of exposing children to activism can bring on anxiety or fear. What are your thoughts about involving your child in activism? What fears do you have about what your child might see?

_____

_____

_____

_____

_____

_____

Now that you have taken the time to think about these questions, I hope you have some idea about the ways activism shaped who you are as a parent. If you did not have a strong history of engaging in activism with your family, you may have some worries or concerns about doing this with your child.

There is no one way to engage in activism, so remember that you can be creative. Together you and your child can find some unique ways to advocate for change in your community.

Activism and Well-Being

Activism takes many shapes. It can be defined as any type of action supporting a political or social cause, such as engaging in civil disobedience, writing or signing a petition, walking in a march to support racial justice, or speaking out against anti-Black racism (Turner, Harrell, and Bryant-Davis 2022). Activism can also look like speaking to local politicians about issues that impact your community, such as the need to reduce the number of police officers in schools. While it may be scary to expose your child to activism, it is a powerful way to help your child cope with racism in society.

Activism and community civic engagement can promote self-preservation and act as resistance to oppressive systems. Using activism as a learning tool helps reduce the stress that your child may experience as a result of encountering racial discrimination and oppression. While there are different types of activism, engaging in these activities with your child can play a significant role in promoting positive self-esteem, resilience, and racial socialization (Hope et al. 2020).

Engaging in activism with your child has some potential harms and risks, such as exposure to violence and negative emotions. When considering which activities to engage in with your child, it can be important to consider whether the event is child friendly. Getting involved in child-friendly activism may include participating in a project to write letters to politicians, going to an educational event at a museum, or helping to raise money or donations for a social justice cause. Events like these involve a low risk of violence.

The questions that follow can help you prepare to engage in activism with your child and make a plan to cope when challenges arise.

What organization or individuals are hosting the event? Do you know them well?

_____

_____

_____

_____

_____

Will police be present at the event? How will you support your child if they have fears about the police?

_____

_____

_____

_____

Is the event child friendly?

_____

_____

How will you support your child if violence occurs or escalates at the event?

_____

_____

_____

_____

What is your plan for leaving the event?

_____

_____

_____

_____

_____

_____

If you find it difficult to answer these questions or don't know how you could support your child, I would encourage you to consider lower-risk activities, such as donating money or supplies to help support a cause. Be mindful of your starting point as a family and your ability to help your child manage their emotions. As your child gets older and you're more comfortable, you can begin to shift to other activism activities, such as attending a protest together.

Ask Dr. Earl

A parent asks...

My neighbor decided to take their child to a Black Lives Matter protest after a local teen was racially profiled while leaving a college prep study group. While I support activism, I am not sure if it is a good idea to take my ten-year-old son to the upcoming demonstration at the mayor's office. What is the appropriate age for children to be involved in activism by attending a protest or rally?

And I answer...

Children tend to develop awareness of racial issues at an early age through observing events in the community. While each child is different, activism may help increase your child's awareness of racial injustice and increase their racial socialization. Children as young as age eight have the cognitive abilities to process events and make connections about how activism helps fight injustice. Exposing your child to activism in their community can create teachable moments that help give them the language to discuss injustice. This exposure will help instill civic engagement in your child and create resilience.

Before making a decision about taking your child to a protest, it is important to have a sense of the nature of the protest. Will it be peaceful? Is there potential for violence? Answering those questions will help you make an informed decision. If you anticipate any violence or potentially traumatizing situations, it may be better to not take your child, as the experience may create more stress for your child.

Factors That Promote Resilience

In 2022, I coauthored an article on the Black Love, Activism, and Community (BLAC) model in the *Journal of Black Psychology*. This model describes how engaging in activism as a Black American can be helpful in preventing mental health difficulties that may result from anti-Black racism and discrimination (Turner, Harrell, and Bryant-Davis 2022). According to the BLAC model, there are four culturally based protective and resilience factors:

Interpersonal relationships: Activism creates opportunities for connection and maintaining relationships with family, friends, and the community, and it often goes hand-in-hand with spirituality.

Spirituality: In the Black community, religious and spiritual communities such as churches often initiate engaging in activism to address racial discrimination. For example, Dr. Martin Luther King Jr. was a pastor who played a significant role in the civil rights movement.

Racial identity: Using activism as a learning tool with your child helps increase their sense of racial pride and helps them feel empowered to address racism in their community.

Artistic expression: Forms of artistic expression such as visual arts, dance, music, and poetry can help prevent the suppression of emotions or silencing that can occur when children experience racial discrimination (Turner et al. 2022). You can use artistic expression with your child as a way to help them release some of the stress or emotional difficulties they hold in their bodies.

This chart provides some examples of culturally based factors for coping and resilience. In the column on the right, add any activities you would do with your child (Turner, Harrell and Bryant-Davis 2022).

Resilience Factors	Examples	Activities You Would Do with Your Child
Interpersonal relationships	Social support and having connections with your community, neighbors, family, and friends	
Spirituality	Religious coping, faith, having purpose in life, relationships to God/Spirit, and connecting with the church	
Racial identity	Having a sense of belonging to your racial or ethnic group; this can be strengthened by sharing positive aspects of your race, such as music, dance, history	
Artistic expression	Creative expression such as music, dance, theater, poetry, and movement (sports, yoga, and gardening)	

Activism and Race Consciousness

Critical consciousness is a framework grounded in the work of Brazilian educator and philosopher Paulo Freire's (2000) concept of *conscientização*, or the process by which marginalized individuals identify and take action to challenge social inequities. In other words, reflecting on your race and racial injustice helps you become more aware that steps need to be taken to address inequity through activism.

To overcome racial discrimination in society, you can help your child use their strengths, knowledge, and racial identity to heal from injustice. Increasing your child's race consciousness helps them examine racial discrimination and oppressive systems, develop confidence to challenge inequities, and engage in social action through activism.

Building on research focused on sociopolitical development, there are five stages to consider to increase race consciousness (Watts, Griffith, and Abdul-Adil 1999).

Acritical stage: Children in this stage are unaware of oppression and do not actively engage in activism. They typically view the world as fair and just, and may have a fairly unbiased opinion of those who are racially different from themselves. If your child has some awareness of racism or how people are treated differently because of their race they may have progressed to a later stage.

Adaptive stage: In this stage, children have a limited understanding of oppression and engage in little to no critical action. They lean toward having a color-blind view of the world and believe that everyone is treated the same. Their racial beliefs are described as minimizing or ignoring the fact that race and racism exist in society (Neville et al. 2005).

Precritical stage: This stage marks the beginning of critical consciousness (or having an awareness that race influences how people are treated). Children in this stage question racial injustice and unfair treatment of themselves and others who experience oppression. They may also begin to engage in activism to address racial discrimination. In this stage, your child may have some understanding about racism, making it a good time for you to help them identify ways to engage in activism.

Critical stage: Children in this stage regularly engage in critical reflection, feel empowered to enact change, and participate in actions to promote justice and uproot oppressive systems. They will begin to desire engaging in more activism and may ask to attend protests with you.

Liberation stage: This final stage includes ongoing and regular awareness of oppression, and a desire to take action to change laws and practices that disadvantage people due to their race. While this stage may describe the reality of older children, you can still play an important role in helping your child speak out against oppression.

Understanding all of these stages of race consciousness are useful for your journey as you engage in activism and racial socialization with your child.

Race Consciousness and Your Child

Now that you have learned about race consciousness, the next step will be to consider which stage your child is in. As you reflect on the statements that follow, consider how much you have talked with them about race and racism. It may also help to think about any situations where they have witnessed or experienced racial discrimination.

Circle T (True) or F (False) for each statement. At the end of the activity, you can determine your child's stage.

T   F   1. My child has never observed or experienced racism.

T   F   2. My child views the world as fair.

T   F   3. My child has an awareness of their Black identity.

T   F   4. My child recognizes when they or other Black kids are treated differently.

T   F   5. My child understands racism.

T   F   6. My child and I have discussed activism.

T   F   7. My child has asked to, or has taken action to, fight oppression or injustice.

Now that you have answered the questions, take a moment to consider which stage of race consciousness may represent your child. If you circled True on 1 and 2, your child may be at the acritical stage. If you circled True on 2 and 3, and False on 4, your child may be at the adaptive stage. If you circled False on 2 and True on 4, your child may be at the precritical stage. If you circled True on 3, 4, 5, and 6, your child may be at the critical stage. If you circled True on 3, 4, 5, 6, and 7, your child may be at the liberation stage.

You may think your child is actually at a different stage from the one suggested by your responses. If so, write down the stage you think they are at, and explain why you chose that stage.

_____

_____

_____

_____

_____

_____

In your ideal world, what could you do to support your child in increasing their race consciousness?

_____

_____

_____

_____

_____

Younger children are often at either the acritical, adaptive, or precritical stage. Given their age, most young children will have an awareness of their race but may not fully understand how people are treated differently based on their race. However, if they have encountered some discrimination or witnessed it in your community they may already have some level of awareness about injustice. At this point in the workbook, I encourage you to use this information to help you better understand your child. The more you engage in activism, the more you increase your child's race consciousness, which is an important part of building resilience.

Activism and Racial Literacy

Over the years, Black people have engaged in activism to help create a better life for our families and communities. Doing this work is helpful to change racist practices and policies that marginalize us as Black people. Engaging in activism also teaches your child that when society attempts to oppress you or your community you can take some critical actions to promote change. In the United States, Black and African American people have engaged in activism to obtain voting rights, help desegregate schools and other public spaces, and reduce housing segregation.

Racial literacy is an important part of engaging in activism. Psychologist Howard C. Stevenson (2014) describes racial literacy as involving three core coping skills: (1) the ability to understand situations that involve racial discrimination, (2) the ability to manage the stress caused by negative racial encounters, and (3) the ability to resolve the racial encounter. Strengthening their racial literacy helps children gain a better understanding of how racism impacts their community and also helps promote their resilience to racial stress—that is, their ability to overcome emotional challenges that may result after witnessing or experiencing racial discrimination.

Racial literacy and racial socialization are both helpful tools for you to process incidents of discrimination with your child. Although you may be tempted to use hypothetical situations in talking with your child, they may not be able to grasp those hypotheticals because their brain is still developing. According to psychologist Jean Piaget's theory of cognitive development (1950), children between the ages of three and eight have a limited ability to make assumptions about situations that are abstract or not directly observable. In other words, young children may struggle to understand what they can't see. Activities such as reading picture books or going to a museum exhibit can make it easier to help them process information and promote racial literacy.

In their work, psychologist Riana E. Anderson and her team highlighted how parental involvement in racial literacy and racial socialization plays a significant part in helping Black youth adapt following discrimination (Anderson et al. 2021). For example, when Black parents report feeling confident in engaging in racial socialization, their confidence helps reduce the risk of negative psychological stressors, such as racial stress, for their child. It is helpful to remember that your ability to feel competent in engaging in racial socialization is also an important part of that socialization. You can build your confidence and competence by preparing yourself through increasing your own knowledge before doing this work with your child. When you feel that you have the skills to talk with your child about racial discrimination, you are modeling for your child that it is healthy to talk about your Black identity. These tips can help you feel more confident, as can the resources listed at the end of this book:

- Visit trusted websites for information that can help you explore racism, the history of Black people in America, and cultural identity.

- Visit your local library or book retailers to find books to read and discuss with your child about their cultural heritage and racial justice.

- Connect with local volunteer organizations, churches and religious organizations, or activist groups in your community to stay updated about opportunities to support causes that fight injustice and oppression.

Gauging Your Comfort Level with Activism

When you engage in activism, you are actually using racial literacy as a way to help shine the light on how work can be done to address discrimination in your community. Instead of trying to create hypothetical scenarios to talk with your child about confronting racism, activism offers firsthand learning experiences for you and your child that promote resilience.

If you have some reluctance about engaging in activism with your child, it is important to start with small steps you feel comfortable with—donating to a cause, writing a letter, or reading books on social justice or activism together. After engaging in low-risk activities like these, you may feel more confident; then you can progress to other activities such as attending rallies or protests with your child.

Many parents have concerns about engaging in activism with their child. Using the questions below, think about the pros and cons of engaging in activism. This is a chance for you to think about what is most important for engaging in activism to promote racial literacy with your child.

Describe the benefits of engaging in activism with your child. How will it help promote racial literacy? What do you hope they will learn?

_____

_____

_____

_____

_____

Describe your concerns about engaging in activism with your child.

_____

_____

_____

What challenges might you face engaging in activism?

_____

_____

How would you respond to those challenges?

_____

_____

Based on your opinion, should you consider low- or high-risk activism?

_____

_____

How will you take care of your own emotions? What self-care practices would help you cope?

_____

_____

_____

Choosing Your Form of Activism

There are different types of activism you can consider with your child. Low-risk activism—donating money, organizing social media campaigns, or writing letters to politicians—has been found to increase resilience and positive mental health. If you have concerns about engaging in activism with your child, you may want to consider some type of a low-risk activism activity. If you are considering engaging in high-risk activism activities—protests, attending demonstrations, or engaging in civic disruption—it is important that you take some time to plan in advance in the case the event becomes violent.

In chapter 4, we discussed critical consciousness—the process by which individuals identify and take action to challenge social injustices. Critical consciousness is created through both low- and high-risk activism. I encourage you to consider ways to engage in activism with your child, as it can be an important step toward helping your child cope with racial discrimination.

The worksheet that follows will provide an opportunity for you and your child to review different activism activities and select those that you would like to do as a family. Before you involve your child in the discussion, consider which activities you are most comfortable doing; then check the box next to the activities you may want to try with your child. Work with your child to decide which one or two activities you would like to do; there is also space to add your own ideas. In the column on the right, you can make notes about the events you might attend or organizations you might work with.

Choosing Your Activism Activities

Low-Risk Activities	Interested in Trying?	Notes
Writing a letter to local or national politicians		
Attending a meeting with school staff and teachers		
Sending an email about an injustice or incident of racism		
Creating a donation website to support racial justice		
Hosting an art show focused on equity, diversity, or liberation		
Other:		
Other:		

High-Risk Activities	Interested in Trying?	Notes
Attending a protest or rally		
Attending a march about injustice		
Engaging in civic disruption (for example, blocking highway traffic)		
Attending the boycott of a business		
Other:		
Other:		

Now let's think about what forms of activism will work best for you and your child. The prompts that follow offer some questions that you can answer alone or with your child.

Before you begin, I encourage you to think about your child's emotional awareness and development. This will help you consider what type of activism activities may be appropriate. For example, if your child has a difficult time expressing their feelings or understanding others' feelings, you may want to consider more low-risk activism activities. On the other hand, if your child is older, they may be prepared to engage in some high-risk activities. The most important thing to consider is that you should select the activities that you and your child feel comfortable doing together.

How easy is it for your child to verbalize their emotions?

_____

_____

Using the list of the low- and high-risk activism activities above, which activities are you and your child considering?

_____

_____

_____

What are the risks you may encounter?

_____

_____

How do you need to prepare yourself and your child? For example, if you decide to attend a protest you may want to consider your exit plan if violence escalates.

_____

_____

_____

_____

Finally, talk with your child about the purpose of the activism activities and how those activities help to address racial discrimination. Try to gauge their interest in each activity. This is an important part of the racial socialization process.

• *The Case of Robin*

Robin is a thirty-eight-year-old Jamaican American woman. A few years ago, she got a divorce from her husband, and they are currently co-parenting their two children, ages seven and eleven.

For many years, Robin has been a member of a local civic organization that often engages in activism and volunteers in the community. After the killing of an unarmed Black person by a police officer, Robin wanted her kids to join her while she engaged in activism against police violence. She spoke with her ex-husband about getting their kids involved, and they came to an agreement that the children were not old enough. They also believed that the children didn't have much awareness about police violence, so they wanted to start by having conversations with them about racial bias. Rather than attending a protest, they read a book together and then donated goods to support those protesting.

Robin and her ex-husband decided to engage in low-risk activism by donating goods to help the cause. They also decided to engage in racial literacy by talking with their children about bias and injustice. While those are two ways to handle the situation, they are not the only ways. For example, Robin could have talked with her children about police bias, explaining that people are sometimes treated unfairly because they're Black. She could have ended the discussion with her kids by talking about how people are engaging in activism to improve police-community interactions.

Take a moment to reflect on Robin's experience, and then respond to the questions that follow. This is an opportunity for you to think about Robin's family and how you might address a similar scenario with your child.

How did Robin's experience with activism influence her decision to engage in low-risk or high-risk activism?

_____

_____

_____

_____

Would you make the same decision Robin did if it were your child? Why or why not?

_____

_____

_____

_____

How could Robin and her ex-husband use racial socialization to help their children?

_____

_____

_____

_____

Activism as a Tool for Coping

Sometimes children can feel powerless when they encounter or witness racism. If you have personally experienced racism, you have probably felt powerless, angry, depressed, or anxious at some point. Negative thoughts or emotions are only natural following these types of experiences.

One way to channel those emotions is by engaging in activism. Activism helps prevent feelings of hopelessness and create systemic change, so when you engage in activism with your child it helps improve their mental health and promote their resilience. Taking action will give your child some confidence in fighting oppressive systems, and they will begin to have a better outlook on their future.

As you may know from your own childhood experiences, parents have a huge impact on how their children think and behave. You can probably look back on your own life and point out the many ways your parents shaped who you were as a child, as well as who you are now as a parent. The thing to remember when trying to engage in activism to promote resilience is that this action requires your effort. Your effort will be helpful to model behaviors for your child. Efforts will also be necessary to help your child work through experiences in life. This will help your child increase resilience and reduce stress, anxiety, and other negative emotions. Using the prompts below, think about your own history of engaging in activism.

Describe any activism you engaged in as a child or as an adult.

_____

_____

_____

_____

_____

_____

How did engaging in activism influence your mood or emotions? Did you feel more hopeful? Did you feel empowered to fight oppression?

_____

_____

_____

_____

• *The Case of Jessica*

Jessica is a ten-year-old Black girl who lives with her parents and siblings. They live in a diverse suburban community. Her parents came across a social media post about a teenager who was suspended from school because he violated the school's policy regarding dreadlocks. They knew that this had been a recurring issue in many states.

When Jessica's parents learned that some parents in their neighborhood were planning a letter-writing campaign to advocate for a change in the school system's dress code, they thought it was a good idea to expose Jessica to low-risk activism. They believed this would be a good way for Jessica to learn to use her voice to advocate for change. Since they had already started having the race talk with Jessica, they asked her if she would like to write a letter to the school board or if there was anything else she believed would be a good way to help others. Jessica agreed that writing a letter was a good idea and expressed the hope that it would help other Black kids be allowed to love themselves for who they are.

I think that using the low-risk activism activity was a wise decision for Jessica and her family. It can play an important role in giving Jessica some sense of her ability to challenge injustice and unfair policies. I also appreciated that they got her involved and allowed Jessica to decide if she agreed or had alternative ideas. If you're looking for ideas to do with your child in a similar scenario, you could decide on writing a letter or you could discuss activities with your child using the activism activities worksheet.

Take a moment to reflect on Jessica's experience and then respond to these questions:

Would you have responded the same way as Jessica's parents in this scenario? Why or why not?

_____

_____

_____

_____

Try to think of other ways they could have engaged in low-risk or high-risk activism activities to support discriminatory policies against hairstyles. Write down your ideas here.

_____

_____

_____

How could Jessica's parents use this situation to promote pride in her racial identity?

_____

_____

_____

_____

_____

_____

Engaging in low- or high-risk activism is a helpful way to support your child. You can also create a teachable moment by talking with your child about the ways other people engage in activism. This could be another step to begin the process of increasing your child's race consciousness. Finding teachable moments may also be something you want to consider if you have some fears or concerns about taking your child out in the community to expose them to activism.

Using Activism as a Teachable Moment

This brief activity can help your child understand the benefits of activism and learn how others use activism to channel their feelings. To get started, identify an event that will demonstrate an example of activism; for example, a story from the news, a photo, or a video of a protest or march. You could also consider going to a museum exhibit that highlights civil rights and social justice movements.

Once you have identified the example, take some time to talk with your child about it. Let them know the purpose and why people engaged in activism. For example, if you chose a photo of the Montgomery bus boycott, you could talk with your child about how African Americans in Alabama protested by not giving up their seats to white passengers. You could share with them how activism such as the bus boycott led to changes in laws that now allow Black people to sit anywhere on buses.

Take a moment to check in with your child about their thoughts and feelings. Here are a few sample statements and questions to use with your child:

- *Tell me a story about this picture/book/museum exhibit. What do you think is going on?*

- *What emotions do you think this person is feeling? Do you think they're sad? Happy? Angry? Something else?*

- *How does looking at this image make you feel?*

You can use this space to make some notes about your child's responses.

_____

_____

_____

_____

_____

_____

_____

Now that you have explored your child's feelings, you can empower them to become activists or speak out against racial injustice. It can be helpful to share how important it is to take action by protesting or engaging in civil disobedience to improve the lives of people in your community. For example, using the bus boycott, you could share with your child how Black people no longer have to worry about being treated unfairly when they ride a bus and they can sit anywhere they want.

Using the space below, describe your experience using activism as a teachable moment. How did it go? What did you learn about your child that will help you with having more conversations in the future?

_____

_____

_____

_____

_____

_____

_____

_____

This activity is intended to use racial literacy and activism to help your child thrive. This is also important to give your child a sense that racial discrimination can be addressed. Engaging in activism will help instill hope in your child in the face of racial discrimination. This sense of hope is a critical part of promoting resilience in your child.

Engaging in activism with your child can be frightening. However, with time, activism can be a helpful tool to help you and your child cope with racial discrimination. Engaging in activism even just once will have a different effect on different children. Your child's emotions may improve after one time, or it may take longer for you to notice that they have improved. Once you consistently engage in some type of activism, you will notice that your child will feel less angry, happier, and show a stronger sense of self.

Time to Reflect

Using your journal or the space below, respond to these questions to reflect on your experience with this chapter.

Describe your experience engaging in activism and racial literacy. Did you decide to start with low-risk or high-risk activism?

_____

_____

_____

_____

_____

What was easy for you and your child?

_____

_____

_____

What was difficult?

_____

_____

_____

Write about what helped you cope while you were engaging in activism. What did you do for self-care? What helped you support your child? What coping or self-care practices do you need to continue teaching your child?

_____

_____

_____

_____

_____

_____

_____

_____

Next Steps

Up to this point we have discussed the importance of activism to help promote racial literacy and racial socialization, and identify strategies for building race consciousness. As you continue working through these exercises in this book, remember to be hopeful about change and maintain a positive outlook. In the next chapter, we will discuss how mindfulness-based strategies can be used to cope with oppression and help promote resilience in your child.

CHAPTER 5

Mindfulness Strategies for Resilience

To foster resilience, you must help your child use healthy coping strategies to adapt to challenges such as racism. In chapter 3, we discussed how racial socialization is one process to help build resilience. Another way to build resilience is through using mindfulness-based strategies, including soulfulness, to reduce stress. Mindfulness and soulfulness strategies include activities such as breath awareness, body scans, sitting meditations, creative expressions, yoga, spirit-infused practice, and mindful movement (Biggers et al. 2020; Harrell 2018; Kabat-Zinn 2003). These practices can help promote attention to our present-moment thoughts, emotions, and physical sensations. Research on mindfulness shows that engaging in mindful practices improves your physical and mental health, including better sleep quality, reduced anxiety and depression, and improved well-being (Watson, Black, and Hunter 2016; Watson-Singleton, Hill, and Case 2019). Using mindfulness-based activities and soulfulness with your child can help them cope with racial discrimination and help them thrive.

In this chapter, you will

- gain an understanding of the benefits of mindfulness practices and soulfulness-oriented approaches; and

- explore different types of mindfulness-based and soulfulness-oriented techniques that can be used for improving your child's mental health.

Mindfulness and Mental Health

Mindfulness was originally developed from Buddhist and Eastern philosophy and focused on awareness and being alert to the present moment. Mindfulness practices have been used for centuries to help promote relaxation and reduce stress. In modern times, mindfulness has become more popular in Western countries as an intervention to engage in coping and managing mental health problems. For example, mindfulness-based stress reduction (MBSR) programs have been created to minimize pain and stress for people who struggle with anxiety and depression (Biggers et al. 2020; Watson-Singleton, Hill, and Case 2019). Mindfulness-based practices have not always incorporated faith and religion, but religious rituals and mind-body exercises are being adapted to address the needs of different communities, such as African Americans (Biggers et al. 2020; Zapolski, Faidley, and Beutlich 2019). These changes to mindfulness-based practices have helped increase their use and appeal in the Black community.

Although mindfulness practices were commonly used among adults, research has also shown that these practices are beneficial for children's mental health and well-being. Research has found that interventions that used mindfulness practices—such as body awareness, breathing, walking meditation, mindfulness-based coloring, and mindfulness-based yoga—resulted in significant improvements for children and adolescents (Carsley, Khoury, and Heath 2018; Sperry 2018).

Stress can lead to many different reactions. For some children, stress may show up as moodiness, crying, difficulties with eating or sleeping, or feeling tension in the body. Others may have difficulties with focusing on tasks like homework, having low energy, or having an explosive temper. Given the impact of racism on children's mind and body, mindfulness-based practices can be useful for your child to reduce physical and mental signs of racial stress.

• *The Case of DeAndre*

DeAndre is a ten-year-old African American boy who lives with his parents in Southern California. He attends a private school where the majority of the students identify as European American, but he hasn't had problems with overt racism from his classmates or teachers. This year, he decided to join the soccer team because one of his friends who was on the team wanted him to play so they could spend more time hanging out. DeAndre was excited to join the team, and his parents supported his decision. They were also a little nervous about him joining the team since he would be the only Black player.

After several weeks of practice, it was time for their first soccer game. DeAndre arrived at the soccer field with his parents. While his parent went to find seats, he ran over to the team to get ready for the game. Before the game started, one of the other players walked over to DeAndre and said, "Bro, you know you're our servant this year." DeAndre didn't make a big deal of the comment and went ahead with warm-ups. The team ended up winning the game and everyone had a good time celebrating.

A few days later, DeAndre was at school and the same kid from the soccer team walked up to him and said, "Hey servant, don't forget to get my backpack and bring it to practice after school." DeAndre had a weird feeling in his gut and felt a bit uncomfortable. He just shook it off and finished the rest of the school day.

At practice, he had a hard time focusing. When he got home that day, his parents noticed that he didn't seem like himself so they decided to check in with him. DeAndre told them that one of the players on the team was making racist comments. As they continued the check-in, they recognized how much the experience was impacting their son. They decided to support him in the moment by engaging in a mindful breathing activity together. This activity helped him calm down, and he was able to sleep without any problems.

After DeAndre went to bed, his parents discussed how they wanted to move forward by bringing the issue up with the school. The next morning, when DeAndre told his parents he felt nervous about going to practice, they briefly shared with him the need to address this with the school so that DeAndre and other students wouldn't have to experience this type of hate. To temporarily help, his parents encouraged him to try using his mindful breathing before practice started.

In DeAndre's case, his parents were able to learn about what he was experiencing through their regular check-in. Recognizing that his emotions were different than normal was a warning sign for them to take a pause and ask, "Hey, is everything okay?" Once they were able to better understand what was going on with DeAndre, they could decide on the best actions to support him. His parents had learned about mindful breathing and decided that it might be a good way to help DeAndre regulate his emotions and body. In stressful situations our bodies tend to respond by having physical symptoms of stress, such as muscle tightness or changes in our breathing patterns. The use of mindful breathing is one technique that can help with regulating difficulties such as racial stress.

Take a moment to reflect on DeAndre's experience, and then respond to the journal prompts that follow.

How might you respond if you learned that your child was experiencing racism at school or in the community? Describe how similar or different your actions would be compared to DeAndre's parents.

_____

_____

_____

_____

_____

_____

How could his parents have supported him in practicing mindful breathing at school or home?

_____

_____

_____

Engaging Your Child

As you use the mindfulness strategies that follow, make sure that your child is invited to participate in selecting which activities they might enjoy. This involvement will help get them engaged in the activity or mindfulness practice. Some children may be reluctant to try these practices or may outright refuse to engage in them. If you find that your child is reluctant to try something new or a practice you suggest, it may help to use rewards to reinforce their attempts to try the activity. If they do try the activity willingly, it could also be useful to praise them for doing a good job by giving them a high five. It can also help to model the use of these practices for your child. When you attempted to get your child to try a new food, you probably tasted it first to show them it was good. Well, the same action can apply to teaching your child to use mindfulness practices. It may actually be easier to motivate your child if you both do the activity together when you first start. You can have the child do the activity alone once they know what to do and they are self-motivated.

Mindful Breathing

Mindful breathing is noticing your breath as it is naturally occurring in the moment. It helps promote a sense of relaxation and feelings of calmness; it can also help release muscle tension and make falling asleep easier. When you teach this technique to your child, be aware that as they begin to focus on their breath, it might change in some way, perhaps getting deeper or shallower.

Before you start, take a moment and say to your child, "Notice your breathing. What is it like?"

Now tell your child: "Focus on your breathing just as it is. Don't try to take deep breaths."

Give your child thirty to sixty seconds to just notice their breathing. If you choose, you can set a timer on your phone for one minute.

Encourage your child to breathe normally and just focus on being aware of their breathing pattern.

As your child continues to breathe, tell them: "Pay attention to your nose and mouth. Which do you use to breathe in? What about breathing out?"

Now tell your child: "Notice your body while you breathe. Notice your belly rise and fall." If you want to, you can ask your child to place one or both of their hands on their stomach and feel the movement.

Tell your child: "Notice your mind while you breathe." As they breathe, encourage your child to say, "Breathing in, I calm my mind and body; breathing out, I release all I hold in my mind and body."

If you notice that your child has difficulties focusing on their breathing and gets distracted, you can encourage them to count each breath. Do this for a count of five: "Breathing in one, breathing out one; breathing in two, breathing out two…"

Repeat this breathing exercise for about five minutes. If you notice that your child is not calmer or they don't say they feel more relaxed, you can continue for a few more minutes. As you conclude, remind your child to notice their breath and body.

Here are a few questions you can ask your child after you finish (Biegel 2017). You can use the spaces below to write down their responses. As you continue using this technique, you can also see how their responses may change over time.

What did you notice when you did this?

_____

_____

_____

_____

_____

Did you feel distracted by thoughts or feelings?

_____

_____

What did you notice as your breath flowed through your entire body?

_____

_____

_____

What was your breathing like when you paid attention to your body?

_____

_____

What thoughts did you notice as you breathed? What feelings?

_____

_____

_____

_____

_____

_____

_____

Mindful Eating

Mindful eating is another practice you can do with your child. This MBSR exercise helps children slow down and fully experience food to nourish the mind, body, and soul (Bailey 2011). You may know from your own experience or from observing your child that eating is sometimes used to cope with stress. Personally, when I've had a bad day, the first thing I usually do is to go buy some chocolate chip cookies. While that can help relieve my stress, eating too many cookies would not be a healthy coping strategy.

It's normal for children to overeat as a response to stress. However, if you help your child shift to eating mindfully it will allow them to take a moment to focus on their thoughts, emotions, and body. Try out this mindful eating exercise.

Typically, small foods, such as raisins, are used for this exercise. Some people may use foods such as fruit, jelly beans, or other snacks. You can decide with your child which food to use.

Put the food you've chosen on a plate or napkin. Reassure them that there are no right or wrong answers; they're just noticing things about the food by paying attention.

Tell your child to pretend that they are a space explorer visiting from another planet and have never before seen a raisin (or the food you selected). Ask them to look at the object on the napkin; what do they notice? If they had to describe the object to someone who had never seen it before, what would they say? To help them decide what to say, you may want to prompt them to notice the color, shape, size, and patterns of the food.

Next, invite them to pick up the food and hold it with their fingers. What does it feel like? Is it cool or warm? Smooth or rough?

Ask them to pay attention to what thoughts or feelings they may have about the food. Do they think they will like the way it tastes?

Now ask them to bring the food close to their nose and smell it. How does it smell? Tell them to notice whether their mouth is watering because they are ready to eat the food.

Get them to put the food in their mouth without chewing it. Ask: "How does it feel in your mouth? Is this what you expected? If not, how is it different?"

Finally tell them to chew the food slowly, paying attention to what they taste as they do. They should continue to notice what is happening in their body as they swallow the food: What muscles are working? How does it feel as the food moves down their throat? Suggest: "Think about the food traveling all the way down into your stomach, helping to keep you healthy so that you can grow and be strong."

Repeat this process with the remainder of the food on the napkin or plate.

Next, talk to your child about how they felt during the exercise. The following are specific questions to ask (Bailey 2011):

What did you notice about eating the food in this way?

Did the food taste different than it usually does? (Ask this question only if they've had this food before.)

Were you satisfied with eating the food in this way?

What do you imagine it would be like to eat an entire meal this way?

Mindful Walking

Being outdoors or in nature can be helpful to improve stress and mental health. Mindful walking allows your child to use movement to bring themselves into the present moment. Below is a mindful walking exercise that you can practice together (Biegel 2017).

Choose a path about ten feet long; it can be anywhere you will be safe inside or outside of your home. The overall path doesn't have to be long because you are not trying to get anywhere. The point is being mindful of the movement, not how far you have gone.

For five to ten minutes, slowly walk back and forth on this path. Encourage your child to move their arms in whatever way feels comfortable. Tell them to notice the sensations of actually walking: what it feels like to lift your foot, shift, move, and place your foot on the ground. You might want to encourage your child to pay attention to what causes their leg to lift or to identify what sensations they have in their body. At the end of your path, turn around, paying as much attention to the process of turning as you did to walking.

If you sense that your child's mind has wandered while you are walking, that's normal; it's what minds do. Give your child permission to stop walking. Take a moment to ask your child to pay attention to whatever thoughts, feelings, or other things have distracted them and then continue walking.

Each time you engage in a walking mindfulness practice, try not to evaluate how you did; there is no good or bad way to do this practice. What is important is being aware that you got distracted and starting to walk again.

List a few places where you could try mindful walking.

_____

_____

_____

_____

_____

_____

After you try this mindfulness walking practice, discuss these questions with your child:

What was it like to walk like this?

What was it like walking with no endpoint or destination?

What thoughts did you notice?

What feelings did you notice?

Did you feel distracted at any point when you were walking? If you did, what distracted you?

Ask Dr. Earl

A parent asks...

My child recently told me that he has a hard time sleeping at night after witnessing racism at school. Although the school addressed the issue and no recent problems have been shared with me, I wonder whether mindfulness can help with her anxiety.

And I answer...

When a child is anxious, their mind is racing with many different thoughts. Mindfulness exercises can be a great way to help your child clear her mind and calm down before bed, so she can fall asleep—and stay asleep. One simple way to help your child's anxiety is to include mindfulness exercises as part of her bedtime routine. For example, if your child's bedtime routine is taking a bath, brushing her teeth, and reading a book, you could add a mindful breathing exercise for her to do once she's in bed, or use a mindfulness-based app on your phone to help her relax.

What Is Soulfulness?

There is a strong relationship between mindfulness and soulfulness. Although mindfulness alone can be helpful for you and your child, centering the soul and soulfulness in relation to the mind and heart are important. Soulfulness is particularly relevant for us as Black people because it combines cultural aspects—such as having a focus on community, connectedness, spirituality, and creative expression—and striving for liberation in the face of oppression (Harrell 2018). The soul is the container for our core values and beliefs. It holds what matters to us and what gives meaning and purpose to our lives.

For you and your child to maintain your mental health in a society where racial discrimination is pervasive, it's important to have hope and experience joy in your life. While it can sometimes be hard to do this, instilling hope in your child can play an important role in promoting resilience. Hope and joy are also helpful aspects of resisting systemic racism. Without hope for a better future, many of our ancestors would not have been able to continue fighting oppression or encouraging us to believe that things would get better in the future.

As you work to build resilience in your child, soulfulness can help them experience joy and hope. Soulfulness is defined as a quality of experiencing life in a deeply connected way through practices that center *bodyfulness* (nonjudgmental awareness of your body), heartfulness, and mindfulness (Harrell 2022). Its contemplative practices combine psychological, spiritual, and cultural dimensions of "soul" to inform the creation of practices such as meditation, deep listening/dialogue, movement, journaling, creative expression, and communal rituals (Harrell 2018, 2022). Contemplative practices might also include strategies such as prayer, art making, labyrinth walking, playing and listening to music, creating a sacred space, dance, storytelling, vigils and marches, and dialogue circles (The Center for Contemplative Mind in Society 2022). Psychologist Shelly P. Harrell (2018) describes how incorporating experiences and expressions of soul into contemplative practices can be used to heal from internalized, interpersonal, and societal oppression.

Mind, Body, and Soul Worksheet

Using the worksheet below, discuss with your child how experiencing racism impacts your mind, body, and soul. This is an opportunity to check in with yourself and your child.

After witnessing or experiencing racism, my thoughts are:	My experience	My child's experience
confused		
upset		
hopeless		
other:		
other:		
After witnessing or experiencing racism, my body is:	**My experience**	**My child's experience**
tense or tight		
restless or fidgety		
drained or tired		
other:		
other:		
After witnessing or experiencing racism, my soul is:	**My experience**	**My child's experience**
disconnected		
powerless		
distant		
broken		
other:		
other:		

Soulfulness-Oriented Practices

Soulfulness provides approaches to help your child be resilient to racism by using contemplative practices that instill the idea that while racial discrimination is present in society, they should walk in their greatness and in the power of their ancestors. There are several types of practices you can consider (Harrell 2018).

Meditative soulfulness: guided meditations and visualizations that make "soul" contact; emphasis on themes of uniting and liberating

Wisdom-centered soulfulness: integration of quotes, proverbs, sayings, poetry, lyrics, passages from sacred texts

Expressive–creative soulfulness: journaling, creative writing (for example, poems, stories, lyrics), art making, music, singing, movement and dance, invention and innovation

Relational soulfulness: deep listening and fully engaged dialogue; mutuality of being seen, heard, understood, and respected; honoring human dignity; shared humanity and experience; facilitation of belonging and community

Experiential soulfulness: visiting "soulful" places (for example, a beach, a park, or another natural setting); witnessing the human capacity for inspired excellence

Daily soulfulness: intentional moment-to-moment awareness of what touches the soul; opportunities to bring daily and routine activities "alive" through enhanced sensory experience; infusing passion, meaning, and gratitude into everyday experience and events

Spirit-infused soulfulness: integration of any of the above with explicit transcendent elements (for example, ancestral connection, connecting to the presence of God, spirit, or higher power; religious prayer); facilitation of spiritual connection and experience

Building resilience to life challenges such as racial discrimination requires that you and your child maintain healthy coping practices and engage in preventive self-care. Any of the self-care practices that were discussed in chapter 2 can be beneficial following experiences of racism or discrimination. In addition, working with your child to create opportunities to engage in soulfulness on a weekly basis can help minimize mental health difficulties when you encounter stress associated with racism.

Soulfulness can help reduce stress and promote joy. It is important to plan at least one activity that you and your child can do each week. Using the worksheet below, review the activities and then mark those your child wants to try.

	✓
Soulfulness meditation	
Reading poetry	
Reading Bible verses	
Creating poems on identity or liberation	
Journaling	
Writing stories about joy, healing, liberation	
Listening to uplifting music	
Making art or painting	
Singing	
Coloring	
Writing poetry	
Connecting deeply with others	
Walking mindfully at the beach	
Hiking outdoors	
Creating a gratitude journal	
Honoring your ancestors	
Praying	
Engaging in activities at church or with religious groups	
Other:	

Meditative Soulfulness

Guided meditations are a great way to practice mindfulness with your child. Guided meditations are often led by experts, teachers, or mental health therapists. They can also be practiced using phone apps, videos, or audio online. One useful guided meditation—the Black Lives Matter meditation—was developed by psychologist Dr. Candace Hargons (2022). It combines mindfulness, affirmations specific to the Black experience, and lovingkindness meditation to help cope with racial stress and trauma. This practice could be used with your child to help them affirm their identity, honor their feelings, and be present with their body.

Racism is enduring and we as Black people are not always afforded the right to safety, kindness, and compassion. Using the Black Lives Matter meditation can teach your child to stop shaming themselves into being strong, recognize that feeling numb or having negative emotions are expected, and notice what experiencing racism feels like in their body. Dr. Hargons shares that using this meditation can help reduce internalized racism and promote self-esteem over time. You can find the Black Lives Matter meditation for healing racial trauma on soundcloud.

After you've listened to the meditation, discuss these questions with your child.

What was it like for you to listen to this meditation?

What thoughts did you notice as you listened?

What emotions or feelings did you notice?

What feelings did you notice in your body?

With your child, create an affirmation they can use whenever they feel the need to reassure themselves of their worth; for example, *I am proud to be Black; I accept who I am.* Have them write the affirmation down to use when needed. It may help to write it on a Post-it note to place on the wall or mirror.

Expressive–Creative Soulfulness

Creative and expressive arts, such as dance, poetry, music, and singing are among the soulfulness activities that can be used with your child. There are different types of therapy modalities that use these activities to promote healing. For example, research on engaging in music and dance has shown that they can help regulate chemicals in the brain that improve mood and decrease stress (Sheppard and Broughton 2020).

Culturally, music and dance have been an integral part of the Black community for centuries. When we gather in community with each other, there is often some lively music playing in the background or people dancing to spread some joy. As you think about your own family, decide if some of these expressive and creative practices might be a great way to engage in soulfulness with your child. Below are some songs that may be a good source of soulfulness. You and your child could even make your own playlist to listen to that helps promote positive emotions and resilience.

- "Alright" (clean version) – Kendrick Lamar

- "Break My Soul" – Beyoncé

- "Brotha" – Angie Stone

- "Brown Skin Girl" – Beyoncé

- "Golden" – Jill Scott

- "Just Fine" – Mary J. Blige

- "Lovely Day" – Bill Withers

- "Say It Loud" – James Brown

- "Ultralight Beam" – Kanye

- "Unconditional" – Kirk Franklin (featuring Le'Andia Johnson)

Writing is also a good way to express creativity and help your child cope with stress. Types of writing may include essays, short stories, or poetry. In addition to being a soulfulness practice, writing is also a therapeutic tool. I began writing poetry at a very young age, and it has been a great way for me to express my feelings. I often use writing when working with children as a way to help them get their feelings out. Writing may also be a helpful tool to allow your child to express their thoughts and feelings.

The writing prompt that follows offers a starting point for your child to create a poem related to liberation and healing. Another option is for you to encourage your child to use a journal or piece of paper to share their thoughts by creating their own story about their life or overcoming racial discrimination.

Poetry Prompt for Liberation

Please read the sentences with your child and then invite them to share a word or phrase to fill in each blank. They can also give their poem a title.

Poem Title: _____

Liberation is free for all.

My pain sometimes feels like _____.

So I hide my hurt to continue _____.

When times are hard or I feel stress

Doing _____ helps me fight racial stress.

My hope is _____.

Today I feel my pain but I'm hoping for a better tomorrow.

Spirit-Infused Soulfulness

Although I recognize that there are some Black people who don't view religion and spirituality as an integral part of their life, these values do tend to be common within the Black community. For many people of African descent, religion and spirituality are woven into our daily activities rather than being separate aspects of our lives (Harrell 2018, Turner 2019). Many of us grew up in homes where we often attended church services throughout the week, and prayer was the centerpiece of many gatherings with family and friends.

The importance of religion among African Americans is reflected in the amount of time we spend in church, and compared to other groups, we are more likely to use spirituality to provide comfort, and to use religion for coping with stress-related situations (Belgrave and Allison 2018). For example, we may often use spiritual reframing to cope with oppression and racial injustice by using phrases such as "God will work it out."

If religion and spirituality are important to you and your family, this may be a useful type of soulfulness practice that you can engage in with your child. These practices might include reading scripture, reciting Bible verses, or engaging in other spiritual rituals (attending Bible study or revival). Below is a religious prompt that you can use with your child.

Religion Reflection Exercise

Using the prompts below, take a moment with your child to engage in this reflection exercise. This is a time for you to be present with God or your higher power. The goal is to take a moment to reflect on an incident of racial discrimination and to use religious values to promote resilience.

Write down a current situation that is causing stress for your child. You can ask them: "Tell me about a problem that is causing you pain (or stress, worries, or sadness)."

_____

_____

_____

_____

Ask: "How does that make you feel?"

_____

_____

_____

Identify a Bible verse to read with your child that can help them cope. You can read the verse aloud with them and encourage them to write it down to use as an affirmation in the future.

_____

_____

Here are some Bible verses you may want to consider:

  2 Corinthians 3:17 (for liberation)

  Psalm 118:8 (for liberation)

  2 Timothy 1:7 (for strength and anxiety)

  Romans 12:2 (for hope and uplifting)

  Philippians 4:13 (for strength and overcoming stress)

After reading the verse out loud, ask: "What was that like?" or "How do you feel now?"

_____

_____

_____

_____

_____

Time to Reflect

Using your journal or the space below, respond to these questions to reflect on your experience with this chapter.

Describe your experience using mindfulness with your child. What was easy or difficult for you? For your child?

_____

_____

_____

_____

Describe your experience using soulfulness with your child. What was easy or difficult for you? For your child? Are there specific practices that your child enjoyed that you would like to continue using?

_____

_____

_____

_____

_____

If you used any of the mindfulness or soulfulness practices in the chapter following an incident of racism or discrimination, write about your experience with that practice.

_____

_____

_____

_____

_____

Write down the practices you want to use for coping in the next month.

_____

_____

_____

_____

Next Steps

In this chapter, we discussed mindfulness and soulfulness-oriented approaches for coping. These strategies can help your child's mind and body recover from racial stress. You can also integrate them into your child's self-care routine to promote resilience. At the end of this workbook, you'll find some apps you can use with your child to practice mindfulness. As a reminder, be sure to use these strategies with your child often to (1) help minimize mental health problems and (2) help promote resilience in the face of exposure to racial discrimination. In the final chapter of the workbook, we'll discuss tips for maintaining your progress and identifying when it's helpful to seek therapy for your child.

CHAPTER 6

Maintaining Your Progress

You've probably heard others say that it takes a village to raise a child. Parenting in and of itself comes with its own challenges—and parenting in the midst of racial violence and discrimination adds a heavy burden to the emotional labor you endure.

Maintaining your progress is rarely a solo activity. You may have heard this African proverb: "If you want to go fast, go alone. If you want to go far, go together." One important part of resilience for us as Black people is having a sense of connection with others. These connections help us in many ways, especially when we're parenting a child.

In this chapter, you will

- explore ways to maintain progress and build your own sense of community support; and

- gain a better understanding of when it is important to consider therapy for your child.

Creating Your Village

To maintain your mental health, continue supporting your child, and cope with racial discrimination, I encourage you to lean on your village. Having a strong village can help you by giving you space to talk about experiences that others have had. It can also help you find other ways to parent your child that you may not have considered, ways that can promote resilience in your child.

• *The Case of Tiffany*

Tiffany is a nine-year-old African American girl who lives in a small town outside a major urban city. Six months ago, an African American student at her school experienced racial discrimination by a teacher and the incident was investigated. The teacher is now retired and no concerns have been reported about other school staff.

After the incident, Tiffany's parents noticed that she was irritable and anxious. To help Tiffany, they started engaging in more racial socialization and using mindfulness by enrolling in yoga classes as a family. Tiffany became more aware of her emotions. She was also more comfortable talking with her parents about her identity. Her parents often did a check-in to see if anything had happened at school and to ask how she was feeling. They noticed these check-ins helped her feel supported by her family. Tiffany was also able to make some new friends through the yoga class. While Tiffany's parents initially made changes to help their daughter, they noticed that connecting with others in the community was beneficial to them as well. Building their village and engaging with others in their community provided an opportunity to support other families with similar concerns about their children's well-being.

In this scenario, Tiffany's parents saw the need to increase connection with others to help their daughter. Here are a few questions to help you think about what support looks like and to identify who would be a good fit for your village:

- Think about what helps you feel supported. Do you need time to be together face-to-face? Would it help to speak by phone or video call? What other ways help you feel supported?

- Think about how your village can help with your parenting. Who can be available to support you when your child experiences racial discrimination?

Your village can also play an important role in helping you and your child maintain your resilience when experiencing racial stress or discrimination. As you learned in chapter 3, resilience requires action, so it is important to remember what you and your child need to help you cope and manage your emotions. Your village can be used to talk about the skills you've been working on in this book. You can also turn to your village when you need to decompress or to engage in self-care. Your village can help you create opportunities for your child to learn about your cultural identity. All of those things are important to promoting resilience.

Use the space that follows to identify activities that you want to consider doing alone or with your child to help promote resilience and well-being. You can think back to the strategies and practices discussed earlier in the workbook, such as journaling, mindful breathing, going for a walk, dancing, or listening to music. Remember to ask your child's help in creating their own list.

To promote resilience and well-being, which activities would you find helpful to do with your child?

_____

_____

Which activities would you find helpful to do on your own?

_____

_____

Which activities would your child like to do with you?

_____

_____

Which activities would your child like to do on their own?

_____

_____

Practice Makes Perfect: Maintaining Gains

By now, you are well aware of how racial discrimination leads to stress and emotional difficulties for you and your child. You have taken time to work through exercises on racial socialization and critical consciousness, and you have explored the benefits of activism. Now is the time for you to use these skills and strategies to maintain the improvement you've made so far. This doesn't mean that you won't have hiccups along the way or that you won't need to review the skills from time to time. However, after you have practiced the skills a few times it should become easier for you to go through each day and face the struggles of helping your child cope with racial injustice.

To maintain your progress, it will be important to go back through the earlier sections in this workbook to refresh your memory. Repetition and practice help us learn new skills. Keep in mind that it will be necessary for you and your child to use these skills often before you can do them without looking at the workbook, so don't feel bad if it takes more than once to learn the skill or strategy. I remember when I first started learning Spanish in high school. As a language new to me, it was hard and stressful. I often felt like I would never learn how to use such different vocabulary in the real world. Over time, I had to constantly practice speaking Spanish. Eventually, I got really good at it and even learned how to read and write in Spanish. Once I stopped using the language consistently, I was no longer as fluent as I had been. Basically, that repetition and practice was essential to maintaining my Spanish language skills.

The same thing applies here. While you may not need to practice these skills in the workbook daily, it will be helpful for you to return to the concepts from time to time. This will help you become more familiar with the content in each chapter, and it will be easier to locate certain sections in the future when racial events happen in your child's life.

When I'm working with families in therapy, we no longer meet regularly once their child's emotions and behaviors have improved. However, if the parent or child has challenges using the skills we worked on, they typically schedule a booster session, which is an opportunity to practice previous skills learned in therapy. The time between ending therapy and starting a booster session will differ depending on each family. Sometimes a booster session is one month after termination. Other times, a booster session will happen months or even years later. Over time, it may be helpful for your to return to the workbook or any notes that you wrote down in your journal.

Using the prompts that follow, take a few moments to think about your life circumstance and your child's emotions.

If you or your child has experienced racial discrimination in the past few weeks, write about what happened.

_____

_____

_____

_____

_____

What did you do to help yourself and your child cope?

_____

_____

_____

Did you find it easy or difficult to discuss the racial incident?

_____

_____

Did you seek support from your village? Why or why not?

_____

_____

_____

_____

Your responses to these prompts will help you decide whether you need to review any previous chapters. If you identified difficulty managing your emotions or your child's, it may be useful to review chapter 2 (managing your mental health), chapter 3 (resilience and racial socialization), or chapter 5 (mind and body strategies).

The point bears repeating: in order to maintain gains and promote resilience it can be useful to review the workbook as often as possible. And if things get worse, this may be the time to consider seeking therapy, or restarting therapy if you've used it in the past.

Writing this workbook was important to me because I've heard so many parents express the need for a resource like this. While I hope that it has been beneficial to you and your child, I know that sometimes we need more than a workbook to cope with struggles in our life. Sometimes we also need a trained mental health professional to help us process experiences or practice skills. I encourage you to evaluate your life and decide whether therapy is needed to help you maintain and strengthen your coping toolkit.

Choosing to Seek Therapy

One common myth about therapy is that it isn't for everyone. While I agree that therapy can be more beneficial at certain points in time, I disagree with this myth as a blanket statement. In the Black community, the stigma of going to therapy can be a barrier. The fear of being labeled "crazy" or "a bad parent" often prevents people from going to therapy or taking their child to get help. People who had bad experiences with therapy may decide that they don't want to have a repeated negative experience.

When considering therapy, it can be difficult to find the best fit. Sometimes difficulties arise because you can't find a Black therapist in your community. At other times, there may be a long wait list to get an appointment, or the therapist you want to work with doesn't accept your insurance. Although the process of finding the best therapist may not be easy, I encourage you to consider therapy when appropriate and accessible. Later in the chapter, I will share more information about how you can determine the best fit.

Ask Dr. Earl

A parent asks...

My daughter recently experienced discrimination at school. She said she was fine right after the incident. However, I've noticed that she has been sad and irritable for the past few days. I'm worried that things will get worse and it will affect her at school. Should I look into therapy for her?

And I answer...

First, I encourage you to trust your gut. If you think that your child is having a hard time coping, it's best to seek help. At a minimum, the therapist can assess the situation and recommend whether treatment is appropriate. Another thing to consider is to what extent you and your child are benefiting from the strategies you learned in this workbook. If you've tried using the strategies and think more help is necessary, then therapy would be a good idea. Finally, some children may have a strong negative reaction or even experience trauma after experiencing racial discrimination. If you notice that your child is having difficulties with her emotions or behavior for more than three weeks, working with a licensed mental health professional to help you identify what is going on with your child and what interventions would best benefit them would be appropriate.

Getting Started

One question that I get often is "When is it appropriate to go to therapy?" There are so many ways to answer this. First, I do think it's helpful to consider therapy as a way to better understand yourself and your child. Being proactive can be helpful; even if you're not experiencing stress or emotional difficulties, there's a lot to gain from therapy. It can be a great way to learn different methods of communicating with others or coping with difficulties. Second, therapy is important to consider when negative emotions are affecting the way your child navigates their day. If you notice that your child is having problems with anxiety, sadness, anger, or isolation, and these problems last longer than two weeks, it could be a warning sign of a mental health difficulty.

Once you make the decision to seek therapy, the next consideration is finding the best fit for you and your child. There are some resources at the end of the workbook to help get you started. You can also ask your child's pediatrician or doctor for a referral. They may be able to help you find someone who is in your neighborhood. A trusted friend or family member may also be able to suggest a therapist.

Before scheduling ongoing therapy, it can be helpful to check in with the therapist you're considering about whether they would be a good fit. You can schedule a phone consultation or send an email. Here are a few questions you may want to ask:

- How long have you been licensed?

- What work have you done with children who experienced racial discrimination?

- How often do you get professional training about working with Black children?

- Do you have training in racial socialization or racial identity development?

- What type of activism have you supported or engaged in?

While this list doesn't cover every question, it can be a starting point. When you decide to seek therapy for your child, take a moment to consider what is important to you and your family. For example, does the ethnicity or gender of the therapist make a difference for you or your child? Those can be additional questions to ask before deciding to form a long-term therapy relationship.

Time to Reflect

Take a moment to reflect on how this workbook has helped you and your child. Using your journal or the space below, respond to these questions about your journey through this book.

What did you learn about racial discrimination and its impact on your child?

_____

_____

_____

_____

What was the most challenging part of this workbook? Tell why.

_____

_____

_____

_____

What was the most rewarding part of this workbook? Tell why.

_____

_____

_____

_____

What was the most helpful thing you learned? Why did you find it so helpful?

_____

_____

_____

_____

What do you plan to continue working on with your child? Why did you choose this thing?

_____

_____

_____

_____

Write about any areas in your life or your child's life where you think a therapist is needed to help you process those experiences.

_____

_____

_____

_____

_____

_____

_____

Conclusion: Looking Forward

Congratulations for making it to the end of this journey! I encourage you to give yourself a pat on the back and do something special with your child to celebrate this journey you've taken together. I hope that you've been able to create the space needed to practice these exercises and that you've learned some helpful strategies to promote resilience in your child.

As you close this workbook, remember that it's here to guide you when you need to help your child cope and thrive. I hope that this journey we've taken together has helped ease your worries about having these important discussions with your child. You've worked hard to get to this point, and the strategies you've learned are a good starting point to help you take healing into your own hands and promote resilience in your child.

Afterword

When Dr. Earl Turner, a distinguished psychologist, professor, researcher, and author, contacted me as he was completing *Raising Resilient Black Kids*, and requested that I write the afterword, my knee-jerk response was to gracefully say no, as I had a packed schedule with my own teaching, research, and private practice. But as he described this project, I immediately sensed and understood the urgency of his book. The reality is that even though racism and discrimination have been part of our collective lives since our existence in America, we are now experiencing an unprecedented series of world and national events, including the pandemic, racist and tribal politics, police brutality against Black people, and school districts banning books by Black authors. These situations have had a devastating toxic effect on Black and Brown parents, resulting in increased racial stress. What is most disconcerting is that the Black community may not even be aware of how this racial stress can lead to physical, emotional, occupational, maturational, and academic problems for our children. Given this dire situation, I had no choice but to agree to do my part and contribute the afterword to Dr. Turner's essential and needed book.

Dr. Turner has made it his calling and mission to address and mitigate racial stress in our Black children. His approach is not only based on his clinical acumen and expertise but also on his long years of research which have focused on the mental health of racial and ethnic minorities, their access to behavioral health services, cultural competency, therapy use among parents, and the impact of race-based stress. The passion for his life's work has earned him a reputation as a nationally recognized expert on mental health and multicultural psychology. But just as important, his contributions to the field of racial stress are also legitimized and strengthened by the fact that he is a Black man in America who faces racial stress every single day, as every Black person does, and therefore the urgency and accuracy of his advice and empowerment strategies in his new workbook are evidence-based, powerful, straightforward, actionable, and engaging for both parents and their children.

As you have no doubt read in this book, Dr. Turner is utilizing an exciting Afrocentric paradigm that is based not just on his clinical, research, and academic work but also on the Healing Emotions and Anxiety Through Liberation (HEAL) method. The HEAL method derives from many conceptual frameworks but at its core utilizes cognitive behavioral therapy; in other words, reframing one's realistic and negative perception of a racial or racist incident or trauma into a realistic and positive learning perception, resulting in less trauma and racial stress and a more positive maturational outcome. Former president Barack Obama referred to this method as "teachable moments."

Dr. Turner also utilizes liberation psychology, another key empowerment strategy, not only to help process racial stress by reframing one's identity and sense of being by honoring African and Indigenous cultural practices but also empowering Black identity and increasing resiliency and emotional healing through seeking justice and equity through advocacy and activism.

This book is also an engaging workbook that provides many exercises for weaving in the aforementioned principles of HEAL, CBT, and liberation psychology through charting, journaling, and conversation starters that can keep us on track with the daily struggle of addressing racism, racial stress and the psychological health of our children in a way that does not become laborious, and is excitingly empowering and transformational. Though it is difficult for any parent to attend to the exercises daily, I encourage you to schedule time with your kids and implement the strategies together or check on their progress one or two days a week. By the way, the exercises can be done at the kitchen table, a meeting place, on the run while going to a basketball practice, or even watching a movie together that can stimulate talking points. Also, parents, let me remind you, that you should also be checking in with yourselves and addressing your own racial stress during the activities and exercises, which will thankfully provide wellness and healing for the whole family.

In closing, over twenty-five years ago, I believed it was my mission as a Black psychologist and Black father to write my first book, *Smart Parenting for African Americans: Helping Your Kids Thrive in a Difficult World*. This book became the definitive guide for raising resilient Black children during that time. Therefore, I can confidently say that Dr. Earl Turner's book, *Raising Resilient Black Kids*, will become the definitive guide in raising resilient Black children in this brave new world. This is a book that you can pick up every day for guidance, strategies, inspiration, and strength for dealing with the day-to-day stressors of race in America.

—Jeffrey Gardere, PhD, ABPP
Associate professor, Touro College of Osteopathic Medicine
Author of *Smart Parenting for African Americans: Helping Your Kids Thrive in a Difficult World*

Acknowledgments

I want to begin by acknowledging the land on which I wrote this book. The City of Los Angeles was originally and is still inhabited and cared for by the Tongva, Tataviam, Serrano, Kizh, and Chumash peoples. Without their sacrifices in taking care of this land, we would not have the space to live and work.

My journey writing this workbook has been one of much joy and deep reflection. I was excited about the opportunity to work with New Harbinger to create this much needed resource for my community. At times, writing this allowed me the space to sit with the stress and trauma that we have experienced as Black people in America. By God's grace and the inspiration from my ancestors, I was propelled to push through those difficult moments to create this workbook.

I want to thank the team at New Harbinger for their dedication to this project and continued editorial feedback in the process of developing this workbook. Special thanks to Wendy Millstine, Jennye Garibaldi, and Madison Davis for their grace, compassion, and thoughtfulness in supporting my vision. It has been a great pleasure working with all of you for the last year and a half to complete this project.

I would like to thank my family and friends for their overwhelming support and prayers. Your encouragement and faith in my ability to write this workbook gave me motivation. The phone calls, text messages, and social media memes were also a good source of self-care.

To my amazing colleagues, Drs. Shelly Harrell and Thema Bryant, thank you for your scholarship, mentorship, and community care. To all of those who came before me—Drs. Robert T. Carter, Nancy Boyd Franklin and Anderson "AJ" Franklin, Janet Helms, Helen A. Neville, Howard C. Stevenson, and so many others—I appreciate your humanity in seeing us when others may not have. It is because of you that I am! Your advancements and scholarship in the fields of multicultural and Black psychology provided the soil for this workbook to grow and offer seeds of advice for parents to care for their Black children.

I also want to thank Dr. Thema Bryant for writing the foreword for this workbook. I'm grateful for your presence, wisdom, and humility. Dr. Bryant, you are a real-life superhero! I would like to express my sincere gratitude to Dr. Jeffrey Gardere for writing the afterword. I have admired your work from afar. As a fellow Black male psychologist, I appreciate your commitment to public awareness on mental health and using your voice to elevate conversations around therapy in the Black community. I also want to give a big shout-out to the students and research assistants who have worked with me through my Race and Cultural Experiences (RACE) Research Lab. It has been a privilege to provide you with mentorship. I am grateful for your assistance with my research projects, as well as helping with library research for this workbook. I am excited to call you my junior colleagues. I know that the future of the profession is in excellent hands.

Finally, I want to extend a heartfelt appreciation to my village and friends of Therapy for Black Kids. I especially want to thank my colleagues, collaborators, and social justice warriors Drs. Maryam Jernigan-Noesi and Isha Metzger for their support and for uplifting me as a fellow Black psychologist. As we all work to help Black kids thrive, love for our community, for our culture, and for humanity is central.

Resources

Books for Racial Socialization

- Abrams, Eshe: *My Brown Skin Is Beautiful*

- Byers, Grace: *I Am Enough*

- Celano, Marianne, Marietta Collins, and Ann Hazzard: *Something Happened in Our Town*

- DK: *Timelines from Black History: Leaders, Legends, Legacies*

- Kamanda, Ali, and Jorge Redmond: *Black Boy, Black Boy*

- Kendi, Ibram X.: *Antiracist Baby*

- Oz, Shola: *I Am Whole: A Multi-Racial Children's Book Celebrating Diversity, Language, Race and Culture*

- Palmer, Bedford: *Black Joy: A Healthy Conversation About Race*

Movies for Racial Socialization

- *Akeelah and the Bee*
- *Becoming*
- *Hidden Figures*
- *John Lewis: Good Trouble*
- *Queen of Katwe*

Websites for Racial Socialization

The African American Experience published by PBS: https://www.pbs.org/wgbh/americanexperience/collections/african-american-experience

The History Channel: https://www.history.com/topics/black-history

National Museum of African American History and Culture: https://www.si.edu/museums/african-american-museum

Mental Health Directories

American Psychological Association: https://locator.apa.org

Association of Black Psychologists: https://abpsi.org/resources

InnoPsych: https://www.innopsych.com

Melanin & Mental Health: https://www.melaninandmentalhealth.com/directory-therapists

Therapy for Black Girls: https://providers.therapyforblackgirls.com

Therapy for Black Men: https://therapyforblackmen.org

Mental Health Apps

Abide (Christian-based app for stress reduction and daily religious practice)

Black Lives Matter Meditation (meditation for healing racial trauma)

Blackfullness (mindfulness app for Black people)

Breathe, Think, Do with Sesame (meditation and stress reduction app for kids)

Calm (meditation, sleep, and anxiety reduction app)

Headspace (sleep and meditation app)

Stop, Breathe & Think (mental health and mindfulness app)

Additional Mental Health Resources

Anxiety and Depression Association of America: https://adaa.org

Boris Lawrence Henson Foundation: https://borislhensonfoundation.org

Mental Health America: https://mhanational.org

Mental Health Coalition: https://www.thementalhealthcoalition.org/resources

The Breakdown with Dr. Earl: A Mental Health Podcast

Therapy for Black Kids: https://www.therapyforblackkids.org

References

Anderson, R. E., N. Heard-Garris, and R. C. DeLapp. 2022. "Future Directions for Vaccinating Children Against the American Endemic: Treating Racism as a Virus." *Journal of Clinical Child & Adolescent Psychology* 51(1): 127–142.

Anderson, R. E., S. C. T. Jones, F. T. Saleem., I. Metzger, N. Anyiwo, K. S. Nisbeth, K. D. Bess, K. Resnicow, and H. C. Stevenson. 2021. "Interrupting the Pathway from Discrimination to Black Adolescents' Psychosocial Outcomes: The Contribution of Parental Racial Worries and Racial Socialization Competency." *Child Development* 92(6): 2375–2394.

Bailey, M. 2011. *Parenting Your Stressed Child: 10 Mindfulness-Based Stress Reduction Practices to Help Your Child Manage Stress and Build Essential Life Skills.* Oakland, CA: New Harbinger Publications.

Bandura, A., J. E. Grusec, and F. L. Menlove. 1966. "Observational Learning as a Function of Symbolization and Incentive Set." *Child Development* 37(3): 499–506.

Belgrave, F. Z., and K. W. Allison. 2018. *African American Psychology: From Africa to America*, 4th ed. Los Angeles: Sage Publications.

Biggers, A., C. A. Spears, K. Sanders, J. Ong, L. K. Sharp, and B. S. Gerber. 2020. "Promoting Mindfulness in African American Communities." *Mindfulness* 11: 2274–2282.

Bryant-Davis, T., and S. J. Moore-Lobban. 2020. "Black Minds Matter: Applying Liberation Psychology to Black Americans." In *Liberation Psychology: Theory, Method, Practice, and Social Justice*, edited by L. Comas-Díaz and E. Torres Rivera, 189–206. Washington, DC: American Psychological Association.

Carsley, D., B. Khoury, and N. L. Heath. 2018. "Effectiveness of Mindfulness Interventions for Mental Health in Schools: A Comprehensive Meta-Analysis." *Mindfulness* 9: 693–707.

Center for Contemplative Mind in Society. 2022. "The Tree of Contemplative Practices [Illustration]." https://www.contemplativemind.org/practices/tree.

Freire, P. 1994. *Pedagogy of the Oppressed.* New York: Seabury Press.

————. 2000. *Pedagogy of the Oppressed: With an Introduction by Donaldo Macedo*. New York: Continuum.

Gobin, R. L. 2019. *The Self-Care Prescription: Powerful Tools to Manage Stress, Reduce Anxiety, and Enhance Well-Being*. Emeryville, CA: Althea Press.

Grills, C., D. Cooke, J. Douglas, A. Subica, S. Villanueva, and B. Hudson. 2016. "Culture, Racial Socialization, and Positive African American Youth Development." *Journal of Black Psychology* 42(4): 343–373.

Hargons, C. 2022. "Mindfulness and Matter: The Black Lives Matter Meditation for Healing Racial Trauma." In *Beyond White Mindfulness: Critical Perspectives on Racism, Wellness and Liberation*, edited by C. M. Fleming, V. Y. Womack, and J. Proulx, 98–109. New York: Routledge.

Harrell, S. P. 2000. "A Multidimensional Conceptualization of Racism-Related Stress: Implications for the Well-Being of People of Color." *American Journal of Orthopsychiatry* 70(1): 42–57.

————. 2018. "Soulfulness as an Orientation to Contemplative Practice: Culture, Liberation, and Mindful Awareness." *The Journal of Contemplative Inquiry* 5(1): 9–40.

————. 2022. "Rising Up Rooted: Black Wisdom as Emancipatory Contemplative Practice for Resilience, Healing, and Liberation." *The Journal of Contemplative Inquiry* 9(1): 171–198.

Hope, E. C., C. D. Smith, Q. R. Cryer-Coupet, and A. S. Briggs. 2020. "Relations Between Racial Stress and Critical Consciousness for Black Adolescents." *Journal of Applied Developmental Psychology* 70: 101184.

Hughes, D., J. Rodriguez, E. P. Smith, D. J. Johnson, H. C. Stevenson, and P. Spicer. 2006. "Parents' Ethnic-Racial Socialization Practices: A Review of Research and Directions for Future Study." *Developmental Psychology* 42(5): 747–770.

Jones, C. P. 2000. "Levels of Racism: A Theoretic Framework and a Gardener's Tale." *American Journal of Public Health* 90(8): 1212–1215.

Jones, J. M. 1997. *Prejudice and Racism*, 2nd ed. New York: McGraw-Hill.

Jones, S. C., and E. W. Neblett. 2017. "Future Directions in Research on Racism-Related Stress and Racial-Ethnic Protective Factors for Black Youth." *Journal of Clinical Child and Adolescent Psychology* 46(5): 754–766.

―――. 2019. "Black Parenting Couples' Discussions of the Racial Socialization Process: Occurrence and Effectiveness." *Journal of Child and Family Studies* 28: 218–232.

Lavner, J. A., A. R. Hart, S. E. Carter, and S. R. H. Beach. 2022. "Longitudinal Effects of Racial Discrimination on Depressive Symptoms Among Black Youth: Between- and Within-Person Effects." *Journal of the American Academy of Child and Adolescent Psychiatry* 61(1): 56–65.

Miller, C., and B. Vittrup. 2020. "The Indirect Effects of Police Racial Bias on African American Families." *Journal of Family Issues* 41(10): 1699–1722.

Moane, G. 2003. "Bridging the Personal and the Political: Practices for a Liberation Psychology." *American Journal of Community Psychology* 31: 91–101.

Neville, H. A., M. N. Coleman, J. W. Falconer, and D. Holmes. 2005. "Color-Blind Racial Ideology and Psychological False Consciousness Among African Americans." *Journal of Black Psychology* 31(1): 27–45.

Pew Research Center. 2023. "Martin Luther King Jr.'s Legacy 60 Years After the March on Washington." https://www.pewresearch.org/social-trends/2023/08/10/martin-luther-king-jr-s-legacy-60-years-after-the-march-on-washington.

Piaget, J. 1950. *The Psychology of Intelligence*. London: Routledge.

Pieterse, A. L., N. R. Todd, H. A. Neville, and T. R. Carter. 2012. "Perceived Racism and Mental Health Among Black American Adults: A Meta-Analytic Review." *Journal of Counseling Psychology* 59(1): 1–9.

Sheppard, A., and M. C. Broughton. 2020. "Promoting Wellbeing and Health Through Active Participation in Music and Dance: A Systematic Review." *International Journal of Qualitative Studies on Health and Well-Being* 15(1): 1732526.

Southern Poverty Law Center. 2019. "Hate at School." SPLC, May 2. https://www.splcenter.org/20190502/hate-school.

Sperry, L. 2018. "Mindfulness, Soulfulness, and Spiritual Development in Spiritually Oriented Psychotherapy." *Spirituality in Clinical Practice* 5(4): 291–294.

Stevenson, H. C. 2014. *Promoting Racial Literacy in Schools: Differences That Make a Difference*. New York: Teachers College Press.

Stevenson, H. C., and E. G. Arrington. 2009. "Racial/Ethnic Socialization Mediates Perceived Racism and the Racial Identity of African American Adolescents." *Cultural Diversity and Ethnic Minority Psychology* 15(2): 125–136.

Torres Rivera, E., and L. Comas-Díaz. 2020. "Introduction." In *Liberation Psychology: Theory, Method, Practice, and Social Justice*, edited by L. Comas-Díaz and E. Torres Rivera, 3–13. Washington, DC: American Psychological Association.

Turner, E. A. 2019. *Mental Health Among African Americans: Innovations in Research and Practice*. Lanham, MD: Rowman & Littlefield Publishing.

Turner, E. A., S. P. Harrell, and T. Bryant-Davis. 2022. "Black Love, Activism, and Community (BLAC): The BLAC Model of Healing and Resilience." *Journal of Black Psychology* 48(3–4): 547–568.

Turner, E. A., M. Jernigan-Noesi, and I. Metzger. 2021. "Confronting Anti-Black Racism and Promoting Social Justice: Applications Through Social Media." In *Making Black Lives Matter: Confronting Anti-Black Racism*, edited by K. Cokley. Solana Beach, CA: Cognella Publishing.

Turner, E. A., and T. C. Turner. 2021. "The State of Black Mental Health." In *Critical Race Studies Across Disciplines: Resisting Racism Through Scholactivism*, edited by J. Chism, S. C. DeFreitas, V. Robertson, and D. Ryden, 239–244. Lanham, MD: Lexington Books.

Tynes, B. M., H. A. Willis, A. M. Stewart, and M. W. Hamilton. 2019. "Race-Related Traumatic Events Online and Mental Health Among Adolescents of Color." *Journal of Adolescent Health* 65(3): 371–377.

Watts, R. J., D. M. Griffith, and J. Abdul-Adil. 1999. "Sociopolitical Development as an Antidote for Oppression—Theory and Action." *American Journal of Community Psychology*, 27(2): 255–271.

Watson, N. N., A. R. Black, and C. D. Hunter. 2016. "African American Women's Perceptions of Mindfulness Meditation Training and Gendered Race-Related Stress." *Mindfulness* 7: 1034–1043.

Watson-Singleton, N. N., L. K. Hill, and A. D. Case. 2019. "Past Discrimination, Race-Related Vigilance, and Depressive Symptoms: The Moderating Role of Mindfulness." *Mindfulness* 10: 1768–1778.

Zapolski, T. C., M. T. Faidley, and M. R. Beutlich. 2019. "The Experience of Racism on Behavioral Health Outcomes: The Moderating Impact of Mindfulness." *Mindfulness* 10: 168–178.

Erlanger "Earl" A. Turner, PhD, is a licensed psychologist, and associate professor of psychology at Pepperdine University in Los Angeles, CA. As a nationally and internationally recognized expert in mental health, he has been featured on television, radio, and in print media outlets, including CNN, *USA Today*, *The New York Times*, *Essence*, NPR, *Los Angeles Times*, and the *Dr. Phil Show*. He is former president of the Society for Child and Family Policy and Practice, and has served as a consultant for *Sesame Street*, Instagram, and other organizations on racial justice initiatives. Turner is also founder of Therapy for Black Kids, whose mission is to help promote resilience and healthy emotional development among Black youth. You can find out more about Turner at www.drerlangerturner.com.

Foreword writer **Thema Bryant, PhD**, is a licensed psychologist, ordained minister, and sacred artist who has worked nationally and globally to provide relief and empowerment to marginalized persons. She is a professor at Pepperdine University, and is past president of the Society for the Psychology of Women.

Afterword writer **Jeffrey Gardere, PhD, ABPP**, is associate professor and course director of behavioral medicine at Touro College of Osteopathic Medicine in New York, NY. In addition, Gardere has a private practice in Manhattan, is an ordained interfaith minister, and has authored four books of his own and contributed to several others.

MORE BOOKS from
NEW HARBINGER PUBLICATIONS

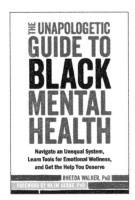

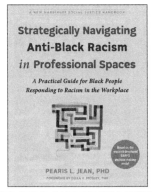
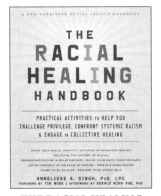

Did you know there are **free tools** you can download for this book?

Free tools are things like **worksheets**, **guided meditation exercises**, and **more** that will help you get the most out of your book.

You can download free tools for this book— whether you bought or borrowed it, in any format, from any source—from the New Harbinger website. All you need is a NewHarbinger.com account. Just use the URL provided in this book to view the free tools that are available for it. Then, click on the "download" button for the free tool you want, and follow the prompts that appear to log in to your NewHarbinger.com account and download the material.

You can also save the free tools for this book to your **Free Tools Library** so you can access them again anytime, just by logging in to your account! Just look for this button on the book's free tools page.

+ Save this to my free tools library

If you need help accessing or downloading free tools, visit **newharbinger.com/faq** or contact us at **customerservice@newharbinger.com.**